Balanced Scorecard

NILS-GÖRAN OLVE AND ANNA SJÖSTRAND

Published in 2006 by   Capstone Publishing Ltd. (A Wiley company), The Atrium,
Southern Gate Chichester, West Sussex, PO19 8SQ, England

Phone   (+44) 1243 779777

Copyright © 2006   Capstone Publishing Ltd

Email (for orders and customer service enquiries): cs-books@wiley.co.uk
Visit our Home Page on www.wiley.co.uk or www.wiley.com

Reprinted March 2006

Other Wiley Editorial Offices

John Wiley & Sons Inc., 111 River Street, Hoboken, NJ 07030, USA

Jossey-Bass, 989 Market Street, San Francisco, CA 94103-1741, USA

Wiley-VCH Verlag GmbH, Boschstr. 12, D-69469 Weinheim, Germany

John Wiley & Sons Australia Ltd, 42 McDougall Street, Milton, Queensland 4064, Australia

John Wiley & Sons (Asia) Pte Ltd, 2 Clementi Loop #02-01, Jin Xing Distripark, Singapore 129809

John Wiley & Sons Canada Ltd, 22 Worcester Road, Etobicoke, Ontario, Canada M9W 1L1

Wiley also publishes its books in a variety of electronic formats. Some content that appears
in print may not be available in electronic books.

CIP Catalogue records for this book are available from the British Library and the US Library of Congress

ISBN 10: 1-84112-708-6 (PB)   ISBN 13: 978-1-84112-708-8 (PB)

Typeset in 9/11pt Garamond by Laserwords Private Limited, Chennai, India
Printed and bound in Great Britain by TJ International, Padstow, Cornwall
This book is printed on acid-free paper responsibly manufactured from sustainable forestry
in which at least two trees are planted for each one used for paper production.

Contents

Introduction to the Balanced Scorecard

A balanced scorecard is a format for describing activities of an organization through a number of measures for each of (usually) four perspectives. A good scorecard documents a strategic logic: cause and effect relationships between current activities and long-term success. As companies and other organizations increasingly depend on their intangible assets, scorecards are becoming a vital tool for management control.

Since its first appearance in early 1992, the concept of the balanced scorecard has been widely adopted as a new approach to management control and performance management both in business and government. A scorecard is an easy-to-understand generic format for describing the ambitions or achievements of an organization. It has proved useful for:

» communicating strategic intentions, as companies increasingly need to involve managers and employees;
» discussing activities that are motivated by strategic aims rather than current necessities, such as development of competencies, customer relationships, and IT, and how these will pay off in the future; and
» monitoring and rewarding such activities.

These aims are equally important in business firms pursuing long-term profitability and in non-profit making organizations, such as government agencies. Compared to other ways of describing what an organization does or should do, balanced scorecards have two distinguishing features:

» one is the almost simplistic format of the scorecard itself, where a restricted number of measures are used for each of four perspectives on a business activity: its *financial* performance, its *customer interface*, its *internal processes*, and its *learning and development*; and
» another is the insistence that perspectives and measures should be "linked". The particular efforts we make in order to learn, or improve our processes, or make customers happier, must be based on our conviction that these will cause future success. The links in a good scorecard will show our "business logic": how doing the right things now is expected to produce long-term rewards. In this way, scorecards translate strategy into terms that are meaningful for members of an organization in their everyday activities.

Brand recognition, competencies, processes, etc., are all part of an organization's *intangible assets*. The benefits of scorecards will be greatest in organizations where these are especially important, and in particular when many organization members are involved in maintaining and utilizing them. Assets such as customer relations, procedures, brand names, databases, etc., used to show up only as costs in planning documents and reports. Gradually, new metrics have been introduced, such as customer satisfaction, cycle times, and brand recognition. A well-designed scorecard provides a unifying perspective for these concepts, showing the intended relation between them and future revenues.

The current interest in scorecards reflects the increasing dependence of *all* organizations on their intangible assets, *and* of the need to engage employees in the pursuit of strategies where the long-term development of such assets is a key to business success. This need will be most apparent in organizations where many employees have customer contacts and where long-term success is highly dependent on interaction with customers and other external contacts. Such organizations need to spend time and effort learning about their environment, improving databases and systems, and creating positive attitudes towards the organization among all stakeholders. Scorecards will guide and focus these activities.

Accepted and widely taught metrics such as "return on capital employed" are of limited interest in such organizations. Take, as examples, two companies that are currently the world's largest in terms of number of employees and market value, respectively, Wal-Mart and Exxon Mobil.[1] The stock market values Wal-Mart at more than four times its equity value. This premium is now sometimes called *intellectual capital*, implying that a reason for this valuation is the realization that there are intangible assets that are not shown on the balance sheet. Even for a company with its own production plants like Exxon, the premium is one and a half time the assets shown on the balance sheet. Owners hold management responsible for developing the total shareholder value, not just the balance sheet, and there is currently a debate how new metrics describing intangibles should be added in external reporting.

Inside these companies the need for change will be even more apparent. Management control is still often based on financial numbers very similar to those in external reports. These numbers give very little guidance to managers whose most important decisions concern customer relations, competencies, brands, systems, etc. Resources spent on these show up as expenses rather than assets. When management control is exclusively financial, there will be a temptation to neglect spending on intangibles, although management rhetoric may identify them as essential in preparing for the future.

So, how should we plan and control such assets, when traditional accounting gives us little guidance, and maybe even a distorted and misleading image? This concerns not only world-famous organizations such as the ones just mentioned above. The problem is even larger for start-ups who have to convince their banks that a first-year accounting loss is really a necessary investment in customer contacts and program code. How can anyone know the difference between waste and essential investments in intangibles when both show up as costs?

A large number of books have been published, with titles such as *Knowledge Management, Intellectual Capital*, and *Learning Organizations* – all attempts to get a grip on how to control the invisible. Scorecards are an essential part of this control. Intangible assets are of growing importance to all businesses, and to government and non-profit making organizations. *Balanced scorecards are important in adding a strategic dimension to management control, but particularly in encouraging discussion about intangible assets.*

Thanks are due to informants at several companies and colleagues, particularly Jan Roy, Carl-Johan Petri and Michael Collins, who contributed their insights. The Japanese cases were kindly provided by Professor Takeo Yoshikawa of Yokohama National University. Although this book contains much new material, parts of it were based on Olve et al., *Performance Drivers*, published by Wiley, and we refer readers to this book and its sequel Making Scorecards Actionable for a more extensive discussion.

NOTES

1 According to the Fortune 500 list published in April 2004.

02

Definition of Terms: What is a Balanced Scorecard?

The *balance* of a scorecard, and the linkages between measures and perspectives, will need to be modified to the specific situation. Scorecards are used as customized communication tools within a management control system. At different levels of organization and for different types of strategy, the mix of different types of control will vary.

A simplified balanced scorecard may look as shown in Fig. 2.1. Some business activity is described from four different perspectives, using a small number of measures for each. The description may refer to the current performance of a business or to its goals for the next period.

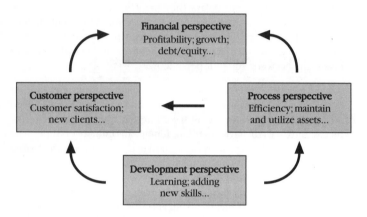

Fig. 2.1 A basic scorecard, with examples of typical contents for each of the four perspectives.

Some would say that this is just another performance report, combining financial and non-financial metrics. But there is more to the scorecard than immediately meets the eye.

» The scorecard is balanced: the four perspectives aim for a complete description of what one needs to know about the business. First, there is a *time dimension* going from bottom to top. Current profitability, etc., may largely be a consequence of what was done last quarter or last year; if new skills are added now they should have consequences for next year's efficiency and financial results.
» The scorecard is also balanced in another way. It shows *both internal* and *external* aspects of the business. It is obvious that a "well-oiled machinery" of internal processes is important in any business, and may not always correlate with external perceptions. On the other

hand, customers' views and the contacts that have been established in the market place are obviously important too. The scorecard shows both.

» Finally, the scorecard is *linked* through cause and effect assumptions. Among its most important uses is to reflect on how strong these linkages are, what time delays they involve, and how certain one may be about them in the face of external competition and change. In Fig. 2.1, links are indicated just between perspectives; in a real case, it is advisable to discuss links between individual measures inside and between the four perspectives.

Scorecards may be used in many different dialogs about any kind of activity. We all reap rewards from what we did earlier, but we also need to prepare for the future; we all have internal routines and external contacts, and we all have to think about causation over time. The introduction of balanced scorecards, however, also means *designing a customized management control system*, whereby scorecards are used to align business activities to the vision and strategies of an organization, it means monitoring performance in the dimensions used in the scorecards, and it means taking appropriate action. This book is about this kind of new strategic, measurement-based control: how it is introduced and how it is used for on-going control.

THE PERSPECTIVES OF THE SCORECARD

When the balanced scorecard was first proposed in 1992 by Robert S. Kaplan, a Harvard Business School professor, and David P. Norton, president of a US consultancy, they used four perspectives similar to the ones shown in Fig. 2.1. There are minor variants in their names:

» financial perspective;
» customer perspective;
» internal business (process) perspective; and
» learning and growth perspective (sometimes: development, or renewal).

Strategic goals, critical success factors, measures, and action plans should be identified for each perspective. This involves means–ends thinking, so there will most certainly be cause and effect relationships between many different factors. The starting point is an overall vision for the company, or the part of it, for which a scorecard is being developed.

The basic logic for how different perspectives relate is usually the following.

» *In order to succeed financially*: we need to satisfy our customers so that they will buy our products; we need to excel at key business processes in order to become more efficient.

» *In order to satisfy our customers*: we need to excel at business processes so that our products will fit the needs of our customers.

» *In order to improve our internal processes*: we need to learn and develop what will be needed in the future in terms of internal processes and value propositions.

A good scorecard should include both measures of outcomes and lead indicators of future outcomes. The latter are called "performance drivers" and describe resources spent or activities performed. By talking about performance drivers we underline that we want to measure those factors that will determine or influence future outcomes. As drivers and outcomes are interrelated in a chain of ends and means, there is not always a clear distinction between them. For logistics, delivery time is an outcome, but for purposes of customer relations it may be considered as one of several performance drivers that can improve customer loyalty.

In their original article, Kaplan and Norton use the term "perspective". Later, a number of companies began to speak of "focus", or "focus area". The two terms carry somewhat different meanings. The customer perspective is about an organization as the customers see it: minimum delays; a pleasant feeling about nice products, or a good product line. Customer focus, on the other hand, may be about customers as they are seen by an organization. What is the market penetration of our products in different age groups or industries? Is the number of our customers increasing? Are we vulnerable from selling to a limited number of major customers?

In this book, the term "perspective" is used, except where some of the case companies prefer "focus". However, in spite of a possible difference between the two terms, they may be seen as interchangeable concepts, both used in practice.

ADDITIONAL PERSPECTIVES

In the authors' native Sweden, many organizations using scorecards have added a fifth perspective: "employees" or "human resources". There are also examples of organizations adding perspectives for "environment" or "partners". It is obvious that the basic format could be adapted in this way, but this sometimes reflects a lack of understanding of the original ideas. In order to keep the qualities mentioned at the start of this chapter (time dimension, both external and internal aspects of the business, and clear linkages) it is probably better to:

» make sure that *employee* measures are included in several perspectives, reflecting their role in the organization's processes, its development, its customer relations, and its financial perspective;

» identify more precisely *how* the *environment* is important in this particular organization. If it is a matter of waste and emissions, these may be measured in the process perspective. If the concern is customers' perceptions, or the environmental effects occurring when the organization's products are used, measures could be included in the customer focus; and

» include *partners* together with customers in a more general "external relations" perspective. Some organizations rely heavily on what is variously called an extended enterprise or a virtual (or imaginary) organization. If this is the case, an organization needs to project a coherent image to customers *and* partners, and these relations should be measured and acted on as one entity.

ON NON-FINANCIAL MEASURES

In a scorecard, a limited number of measures (usually 15–20 in all) are used to describe performance relating to the success factors. With the balanced scorecard the focus is on a deliberately selected set of measures, few enough to keep track of, and this is used to achieve a shared view of the organization's strategy. Although the links are not always shown in scorecard documents, they should be a vital part of the development and use of scorecards.

A measure (or metric) may, in this context, be understood as a compact description of something, expressed in numbers, words, or symbols. Often this description concerns the current state of something or – as a goal or target – a desired state. With this definition, pass/fail and male/female are examples of measures, as well as time to market and churn rate for personnel or customers. Measures facilitate communication about something by enforcing a prescribed format (reminding everyone about which qualities one has agreed are the essential ones) and providing quick overview. This works as long as the sender and receiver of the information share a common understanding of the measures and their context. They need to agree if one or five is the highest grade, they must share a feeling for how much better four is compared to two, and they may need to know the relative distribution of grades. The measures used in scorecards have to be adapted to the knowledge and frames of reference of the people who use them for discussing the activities that the scorecards describe.

This is particularly important because the success of balanced scorecards depends more on their use than their precise design. This is why the following chapters discuss the process more than the look of scorecards. The key lies in finding, understanding, and influencing the cause and effect relationships inherent in the processes of an organization. To achieve this, an understanding of the basic model is important.

BALANCED SCORECARD AND OTHER MODES OF CONTROL

By themselves, scorecards do not constitute management control. However, they are introduced as an important tool for strategic management. In this context, scorecards need to be related to other current concepts, such as "value-based management", "shareholder value", and "intellectual capital". In many organizations the challenge now is to arrive at a suitable mix of financial controls and scorecards.

Financial controls (usually focusing on return on capital) are sufficient only when management is remote and does not have a viewpoint of its own concerning the business logic and success factors. This may be true in conglomerates or holding companies, where the different businesses are viewed just as financial investments.

As soon as control is based on some strategic vision, corporate leaders will need to communicate with management about this vision and its business logic. So-called "*value-based management*" uses revised monetary measures such as economic value added (EVA) to stimulate activities leading to shareholder wealth. Although still predominantly financial, this type of control is not limited to measures found in standard financial reports (profit and loss accounts, and balance sheets). Here, business units may be regarded as long-term investments, where projected cash flow over time is the main focus.

The use of balanced scorecards for control should be seen as "*strategic management*". Here, control metrics should capture the strategic aims and logic of business activities, making it natural to include non-financial measures and to indicate as clearly as possible linkages between actions and metrics.

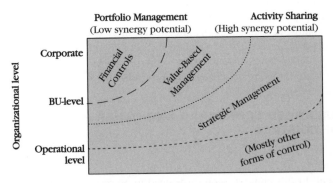

Fig. 2.2 Dominant modes of control at different organizational levels in large, multibusiness corporations pursuing different basic strategies. Adapted from an article by Nilsson and Olve–See reference in Chapter 9.

Figure 2.2 shows this in a highly simplified manner. To the right, where corporations are pursuing synergies, scorecards will be used at fairly high corporate levels – even at group headquarters. To the left, where corporations are managed like portfolios, more traditional controls will continue to be most important. At division or business unit level, however, scorecards will be valuable for communication about visions and business logics.

Financial measures used for control (to the left in Fig. 2.2) will normally be part of the scorecards used (to the right). The design of balanced scorecards involves getting the right mixture of different kinds of control, at different levels in the organization. Scorecard projects easily lead into a reconsideration of strategy and management control.

03

Evolution

The concept of a balanced scorecard was first proposed in 1992 by Kaplan and Norton. As the basic format is quite simple, a number of variants soon developed, both in terms of how scorecards look and how they are used. This means that an organization's claim that it uses balanced scorecards now may mean very different things. We indicate some of the range.

ORIGINS

The idea of a balanced scorecard for business emerged from consultations with companies to identify a planning and performance control process suitable for the 1990s and was first presented by Kaplan and Norton in 1992. Increased dependence on immaterial resources was a major reason why a quest for control tools using metrics other than traditional, financial ones seemed necessary. The time was ripe for a concept integrating several ideas that had gained importance during the 1970s and 1980s, and would develop in parallel with the balanced scorecard.

» Customer satisfaction indices, and the general idea that it was important to monitor value as perceived by customers.
» "Network" ideas of customer and supplier relationships as assets that a company should maintain and develop over time, important for future earnings and consequently an important part of the value of a business. Terms such as "customer base", "partnerships", "alliances", and "virtual and imaginary organizations", emerged at about the same time.
» Process orientation and quality as critical for business success were promoted through acronyms such as TQM (total quality management) and BPR (business process re-engineering).
» Human resource accounting provided the roots for other types of "intellectual capital" reporting, with ambitions to provide both internal and external parties with an improved understanding of the most important assets of an organization.

These ideas could be integrated into the customer and process perspectives. For the development (learning and growth) perspective, there were comparatively fewer suggestions.

The use of non-financial measures had a history going back much further. Local information systems (in a production unit or a sales department) attracted the attention of accounting research in the 1980s, but had always existed. Large corporations have used non-financial numbers in a systematic way for at least 50 years. And, as Kaplan and Norton pointed out, there will always be hundreds of numbers which are used in an organization that should not be included in scorecards. The scorecard idea was essentially to articulate strategy through a particular format, integrating a highly restrictive selection of metrics.

An important feature of the balanced scorecard format is the idea of "drivers" and "outcomes", that is, the scorecard as a description of business logic. The scorecard should depict a set of hypotheses on which the business is built, for instance, that improvements in processes will be rewarded with more customers and cause increased revenues. Such means–ends relationships by themselves are, of course, nothing new, but the insistence that they should form an important part of what is otherwise essentially a compact key numbers report may have been.

VARIANTS

At the same time as the balanced scorecard, a number of similar models were suggested. Some users of the balanced scorecard concept have departed from the original model in certain ways, sometimes reflecting influences from alternative models.

» In Scandinavia in particular, introducing an employee or human resource perspective has become almost standard. This was propagated by Skandia, an insurance company, whose "Navigator" consequently consists of five perspectives. The four non-financial perspectives were linked to the component parts of Skandia's "intellectual capital", human capital, customer capital, innovation capital, and process capital.

» In some organizations it was the development (learning and growth) perspective that was changed into an employee perspective, arguing that development was essentially a matter of human competence. The resulting four perspectives were then seen as a stakeholder model (owners, customers, and employees, with processes as the odd one out). The stakeholder logic, however, seems to be at odds with the cause and effect idea of the basic scorecard format.

» Utilizing previously existing metrics, some organizations limited their scorecards to a human resource perspective, a customer perspective, and a financial perspective, tracing the effects of improved competencies and attitudes on customer satisfaction and profits. Neglecting other aspects of processes and development in this way may be

acceptable for some service industries, but in most cases would seem to be a very partial understanding of the scorecard idea.
» Separate long-term and short-term scorecards were tried in some organizations. The benefits from this are unclear. With balanced scorecards, there is an obvious need to have targets with different time frames within each perspective.

Perhaps more important were the variants emerging for *how* scorecards were used. The original idea of a strategic control tool, to be used throughout an organization and based on over-arching strategic concerns, was probably realized in only a minority of cases. Many organizations find it hard to articulate a corporate strategy, and financial measures are usually more acceptable and even sufficient at this level, especially in more differentiated groups. Much scorecard work, therefore, started at division or business unit level, or even lower down in organizations, where non-financial metrics and concrete assumptions about cause and effect relationships were found to be more attractive than traditional controls. Some companies (Skandia again provides an example) even argued that scorecards should be built bottom-up rather than mandated from the top.

Scorecard projects existed which never went beyond an initial articulation of a scorecard, and yet were seen as highly valuable in clarifying strategies. At the same time, other organizations pushed systematic measurement and reporting as the essential part of their scorecard projects. A consequence was that scorecards in some organizations consisted of a set of overhead slides in presentations made by the chief executive officer (CEO), in others comprised elaborate performance measurement routines without much contact with strategy. In some the balanced scorecard project became synonymous with a new software package for reporting numbers that already existed. As will be argued in later chapters, to obtain the widespread and connected use of balanced scorecards without lapsing into meaningless rituals may be the real challenge for scorecard projects.

The relative importance given to the different ways of representing scorecards (see Fig. 2.1 and Figs 6.1–6.4) has a strong influence on how scorecards are perceived, and the intentions in using them. In their books published in 2000 and 2004, Kaplan and Norton stress even more strongly the strategic intent of scorecards, in particular the use of strategy maps. This ties in with our own experience. We often start by establishing a very general understanding of the business logic, by use of strategy maps. For instance, Fig. 3.1 shows a possible map for a new e-business operation, where order fulfillment is performed through a partnership, and the current business logic is to grow through attracting customers to the website. During the "dotcom crisis" there were many reports of organizations misjudging the balance required between an elegant website, really attractive offerings to customers, ease of operation, and reliable order fulfillment. A map like this could provide the starting point for arriving at a good mix of these. (Another example may be found in Fig. 6.5.)

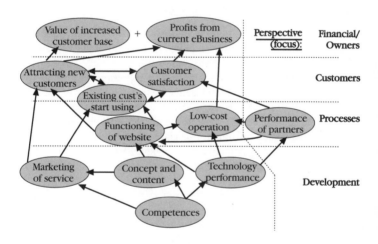

Fig. 3.1 A strategy map for a new e-business venture.

As can be seen from the map, the business owners are interested both in current profits and increasing its customer base. To monitor developments, they will need to keep track both of customers new to the company, how many "old" customers start using the website, and how satisfied they are. Processes include not only an efficient website, but (at least as important) that partners who are essential for order fulfillment perform well. Finally, development of several kinds is needed: concept, competencies, and technology.

APPLICATIONS

A difficulty in establishing the penetration of scorecards is what is meant by "use of" balanced scorecards. In some studies, half the respondents have claimed that their organization uses scorecards or will soon do so, but organizations where management control is totally based on scorecards are much fewer. The fact that most respondents believe that they (should) use scorecards is interesting by itself, as are the difficulties also reported. In fact, there are very many different variants to be found among the applications we have learned about.

» As already mentioned, a number of organizations use scorecards as a format for discussing strategies only, and have not really introduced them as a tool for ongoing management control.

» Some organizations structure plans and reports into four or five perspectives derived from the balanced scorecard. However, they use these only for sorting existing measures to provide an overview, and the resulting "scorecard" does not really derive from any coherent strategic discussion. Although this shows that the scorecard format is generally accepted and attractive, organizations that just use it for sorting pre-existing measures are not expected to realize its potential benefits.

» In some cases, scorecards were introduced as a substitute for budgets, whereas in others budgets and scorecards co-exist. A fairly common ambition has been to combine scorecards with rolling forecasts of cash flow. This is because budgets are perceived to have a dual role: providing performance targets, and foreseeing cash needs. The former role is taken over by scorecards, whereas the latter has to be handled in some other way.

» In most cases, scorecards exist within business hierarchies. Should identical metrics be used at different organizational levels? Here the approach differs. A common method seems to have a small set of mandated measures which should be used throughout, but allow each unit to customize its scorecard by adding some metrics of its own.

» Ideas also differ about how measures within a hierarchy relate to each other. Some organizations (and, incidentally, most software vendors) expect numbers to be possible to aggregate throughout, whereas among others it is the logic rather than the numbers that matters. Some examples: certain measures obviously are easy to combine (like adding profits). But is it meaningful to calculate an average of market shares or employee scores? Has a division necessarily met its targets if the sum of its subunits fulfills expectations, but this hides large differences between them?

» Some organizations have used scorecards for projects – of course in cases where these have a fairly long lifespan. In organizations where projects reach across a normal hierarchy, there may then be targets deriving from one vertical and one horizontal scorecard. Such scorecards for matrix organizations seem to be an area that has yet to develop.

» Scorecards for corporate functions such as IT or HR have been suggested and tried. This introduces the need to distinguish between a scorecard for, say, an IT *department* and the whole organization's *utilization* of IT.

» Reporting performance, in scorecard terms, to the public, in annual reports for instance, has been very rare. However, current suggestions for a richer reporting using terms such as "intellectual capital" often show the influence of balanced scorecard thinking.

» Scorecards for government and other non-profit making organizations are gaining in popularity. This usually requires some reformulation of the scorecard; either the financial perspective is changed into some other kind of "owner's" perspective, or such scorecards have to illustrate in some other way how financial goals are no longer predominant.

A common denominator in all these applications is that the balanced scorecard is an attractive format for discussing human activities whenever there is a need to communicate ideas about causes and effects, and priorities, or to check what has been achieved so far. There is no single best way of using scorecards. However, before starting a scorecard project, it is important to consider what part or aspect of an organization and its activities are in need for this kind of discussion, and who is to take part in it. This should determine the scope of the project, in terms of how large parts of the organization should be included, who should be involved, and at what stages (as a planning tool; for monitoring activities; and for reviewing achievements).

THE FUTURE: COMBINING SCORECARDS AND BUDGETS

In Fig. 2.2, the use of scorecards was linked to strategy and organizational level. In this chapter, "intellectual capital" has been identified as an important determinant. Scorecards are expected be most useful where management and employees need to agree on activities which are strategically motivated and which involve long-term commitments that are "intangible", that is, not recognized as assets in traditional accounting.

As has been shown, the concept of a balanced scorecard has proved influential to such an extent that, now, it is difficult to define any "proper" use of scorecards. Instead, it may well be that the simple format of a scorecard (as a way of describing the activities of an organization) will be integrated into a variety of uses and situations. Maybe even the term "balanced scorecard" will go away, and a "balanced" set of metrics will be considered the natural way of describing the work of any organization?

Based on this hypothesis, we should also comment briefly on the fact that scorecards have been seen, in particular in Scandinavia, as a substitute for budgets. Financial goals will, of course, be part of a scorecard, and the other metrics correspond to the (sometimes unstated) assumptions behind the budget. But most budgets are similar to accounting reports, and budgetary control too often proceeds line-item by line-item, rather than by stressing business logic.

A vital condition for a successful scorecard project is to sort out the relationship between scorecards and other controls. In some cases budgets have been succeeded by two separate routines. As *financial goals*, they have been integrated into the financial perspective of scorecards. As *cash and currency predictions*, their role has been taken over by rolling forecasts that are updated monthly or quarterly. In this way, a mistaken focus on keeping within the "appropriations" of the budget may be removed, but the necessary financial forecasting function is retained. The latter may even be improved, as budgetary tactics will no longer influence the predictions.

Scorecards will also have to be reconciled with other planning processes (market and production plans, etc.). The need of management to communicate the primacy of scorecards has already been mentioned – employees need a clear idea what is more important, to stay within budget or to fulfill what has been agreed and documented in the scorecard.

Management control based on financial numbers tends to be rather similar across industries. It is obvious that scorecards need to reflect the highly specific conditions for each company. Hopefully, what will emerge is a combination of budgets and other traditional controls with scorecards, adapted to each particular organization's quest for uniqueness.

04

The E-Dimension*

Ongoing use of scorecards will require IT solutions. The range of applications and vendors is becoming large, reflecting the very different ways scorecards are used in different organizations. Because of this, it is often useful to rely on temporary solutions at the beginning of scorecard projects, until it is possible to predict how scorecards will look, who will use them, and how.

---

* Co-authored by Michael Collins, Cepro Management Consultants, Stockholm

BASIC REQUIREMENTS

If a balanced scorecard is to play a natural part in an organization's strategic discussion and learning process, it has to be continually updated with current and operationally relevant information. Thus, a crucial question for the organization is how to establish procedures and systems of measurement that collect this information and communicate it to employees and partners.

Whether a simple and straightforward system, based on manual input, or a more sophisticated software solution is chosen, success depends on communicating the right level of information to the right people.

Above all, a balanced scorecard strategic feedback system must communicate strategic-level information to senior executives. But it must also provide information to controllers, market analysts, and many others whose job it is to investigate this information further. It must also funnel information down through the management levels to support individuals seeking information on how their own actions can support the overall strategy of the organization.

FUNDAMENTAL QUESTIONS

Software companies discovered the potential for developing new products at an early stage, introducing applications designed as specialized tools for balanced scorecard projects. Other companies reinvented or extended their existing applications to fit the same needs. However, the market was not quite ready for this kind of packaged application. Initially, organizations implemented balanced scorecards through existing applications, focusing mainly on high-level management and the relationships in the four perspectives: customers, financials, internal processes, and learning and growth. But as the balanced scorecard concept began to gain more widespread acceptance, the market for more advanced solutions also grew and, today, there are numerous specialized balanced scorecard applications on the market.

Any organization that makes the decision to go ahead and evaluate software solutions available today faces quite a challenge, considering the many software options on the market.

The overall questions to ask in the process of establishing procedures and systems for the balanced scorecard are as follows.

» *Should we use software at all?* This decision should be easier to make once potential users have a clearer picture of the scope and purpose of the balanced scorecard and how the information is to be gathered, distributed, and guaranteed.
» *Should we use applications already implemented in our organization?* If so, to what extent do they need to be modified?
» *Should we invest in a new application that fits our needs?* How then do we evaluate the different alternatives on the market?

SELECTING AN IT SOLUTION

First, ensure the quality of the information!

As with any information system, the success of any balanced scorecard strategic feedback system is wholly dependent on the quality of information within it. An organization is not ready to introduce an IT solution until the quality of the information contained in the scorecard has been ensured. This step consists of two elements.

» *Analyzing the measures chosen*: the measures, which are the specific expression of the organization's success factors, strategic aims, and vision, are seldom unambiguous as they stand. More likely, the measures used will be unclear in nature; often, they have been chosen for precisely that reason. Thus, when the different elements of the balanced scorecard have been defined and formulated, the different measures need to be reviewed and analyzed:
  » Are they clearly and uniformly defined?
  » Does everyone agree upon the meaning of universal concepts used to define the measures?
  » Do the measures reflect the strategy of the organization?
  » Is it evident how the different perspectives are interrelated?
» *Ensuring the reliability and validity of systems and methods of measurement*: one effect of formulating new measures of performance is that the organization will have to put in place new systems of measurement. Initially, this may involve a lot of work which will have to be done manually. Thus, the theoretical cost of measurement

will be understated; new information for decision-making must be analyzed constantly and its utility weighed against the additional cost of preparing it:

» How adequate are today's methods and systems of measurement for what they will be required to do in the future?
» Is it economically justifiable to measure everything?
» At what intervals should the different measurements be taken?
» Who will be responsible for the respective measures?

Evaluating the alternative solutions

There are some basic requirements to be considered when evaluating the different options for a balanced scorecard IT solution. Above all, the information provided by the system must be:

» presented in a communicative manner – in numbers, figures, diagrams, or multimedia which facilitates an overview;
» presented in a user-friendly environment – simple, familiar interface;
» easy to access – the people who need the information must be able to obtain it wherever they are; and
» collected and measured in a cost-effective manner – measures of "soft" data often require new instruments of measurement. The cost of measurement must not exceed the utility of the measures.

Another question to be asked when choosing an IT solution is: For whom is the information intended? Sometimes managers would like to see widespread distribution of scorecards in order to provide a shared view of different businesses, and in other cases the scorecard may contain very sensitive information, intended only for the eyes of executive management.

A third dilemma facing balanced-scorecard implementers is how to select a tool which will not be too expensive during the early, and simpler, stages of the implementation, but will meet requirements when the scorecard starts to grow in the organization. Before selecting any software, therefore, it is important to consider how the system is likely to evolve.

The Balanced Scorecard Collaborative[1] has established a set of basic requirements for balanced scorecard applications, based on four areas of functional requirements:

» design;
» strategic education and communication;
» business execution; and
» feedback and learning.

Based on these standards, software vendors may be certified by the Balanced Scorecard Collaborative.

There are three main categories of IT solutions, each one reflecting a certain level of ambition, or a phase in the evolution of the balanced scorecard.

The basic scorecard – the need for a user interface

The first phase of implementation is usually to address the vision, critical success factors, goals and measures of the organization as a whole. This will usually result in a rather limited number of measures to be calculated and reported each period. The system should permit these data to be presented and comparisons to be made between units and over time. The solution is rather unsophisticated and presentations are made in the form of color-coded graphics or "speedometers", often resembling car instrument panels or dashboards (see Fig. 4.1). Data may be collected both manually and, to some extent, imported from existing enterprise resource planning (ERP) systems.

The technical requirements are an underlying database of some kind, but essentially the application can be developed with simple tools such as *Visual Basic*, *Excel*, *Lotus Notes*, or *Delphi*, etc.

Growing the scorecard – creating an executive information system

The real benefit of the balanced scorecard is in influencing behavior at all levels of the organization. This means that scorecards need to be produced for, and communicated to, departments, processes, and individuals. This places a completely different set of requirements on a data capture and reporting system than is needed to compile a basic scorecard. In addition to the form of presentations in the basic scorecard, a tool is needed which allows automatic data collection from various other systems already in place, and furthermore, the possibility of data retrieval from a data warehouse.

Fig. 4.1 Screen from typical scorecard presentation software: ''Cockpit Communicator'', used in Ericsson Enterprise (see Chapter 7 for case study). The software was originally developed by Ericsson and is now spun off as a separate company, 4GHI Solutions AB.

To search for explanations to the development of different key measures calls for a more sophisticated solution than one simply involving storage and presentation of data. The most appropriate technique is on-line analytical processing (OLAP). With OLAP, data are accessible in multidimensional format, similar to an ordinary spreadsheet but maintained in more than two dimensions. Statistical calculations may then be performed to provide trends or forecasts.

With an intranet, this kind of IT solution becomes even more interesting; software need not be stored on the client computer but can be downloaded as needed, or run in a window using a web browser with the help of technologies such as Java. A major advantage of use of the web is that it has become a universally accepted language and communication platform that users have readily accepted. With the web it becomes possible to:

» report cost-effectively and simply on data not easily retrievable from other existing systems;
» facilitate automatic data collection from different systems, as well as a degree of "drill-down" to different levels of data;
» provide a user-friendly, easily accessible tool for data presentation; and
» present results and trends for data in a balanced-scorecard structure as well as comment on the trends and indicate what actions should be taken.

The need for full functionality – developing simulation models

The word "balance" implies an understanding of how the views on the scorecard affect each other, in order to optimize goals. The ability to simulate and model the scorecard provides an opportunity to do so. In the third category of software, simulation models are added. However, these simulations should be regarded primarily as a means of encouraging discussion and consensus on basic assumptions, they are not predictors of future events and results.

By integrating the ideas underlying the balanced scorecard and systems theory, the organization may be observed more dynamically. A "systems view" is inherent in any scorecard, through the idea of linkages over time between "drivers" and "outcomes". Better decisions for the future may be made by use of systems theory and the tools of simulation to test different decision alternatives as a basis for discussing how the future might look.

Specialized products, such as the SAS Institute's *Strategic Vision*, *Gentia*, *QPR*, *Ithink* or *Powersim* can help to illustrate cause and effect relationships, and provide a platform for discussion about how different actions will affect different variables in the system.

TYPES OF VENDORS

In addition to the categories mentioned earlier, distinction may also be drawn between software vendors with different backgrounds, in terms of their other products. Although categories have blurred, there are primarily three different types.

ERP and financial consolidation providers

Companies providing integrated enterprise resource planning (ERP) solutions (for example, SAP) have added balanced scorecard software to their offerings. Customers who want to use scorecards as their preferred view of *all* different types of control data may want to choose this kind of integrated offering. The scorecard software will probably then be an add-on to an existing integrated control system, or may be one of the features that causes a customer to choose a particular vendor.

Designers of popular consolidation tools, such as *Hyperion* and *Frango*, have been quick to realize that much of the data required for calculation of measures already exists in these systems. They have therefore seen it as natural to offer balanced scorecard functionality as well. In cases where more sophisticated analysis is needed consolidation tools provide links to OLAP servers and reporting tools.

Business intelligence providers

Companies focused on database and "business intelligence" software (for example, Oracle, the SAS Institute, Cognos, etc.) also provide balanced scorecard software. Organizations that want to combine their scorecard work with the analysis of large amounts of data about customers or production processes may find it attractive to regard their scorecard software as an add-on to their data warehouse systems. These solutions have the advantage of the flexibility and data-driven functionality associated with OLAP and data warehousing.

Component-based solutions

Several companies offer what they call enterprise performance management (EPM) systems that include balanced scorecard software as an important component (for example, Gentia, ProDacapo). It is difficult to draw strict lines between these and the former two categories, but many organizations looking for a separate scorecard application seem to have preferred these rather less integrated solutions. There are also some companies offering balanced scorecard software as a spin-off from those they developed for their internal use (for example, Skandia, Ericsson).

AN ILLUSTRATION

During 1999 and 2000, several of the leading Swedish pension insurance companies introduced scorecards to facilitate more strategic control. At this time there were important changes in their market, caused by a parliamentary decision to let wage-earners select which pension funds they wanted to entrust with parts of their earned pension rights. Because of this, these organizations needed to focus their employees on attracting these new customers, and provide service to a greatly enlarged customer base.

In one of these organizations, which we will call KMP, the management developed scorecards for the entire company, for its departments and subdepartments. Everyone among its few hundred employees was involved in this exercise. When the new business year, 2000, commenced, the management wanted to give high visibility to scorecard measures, providing access for everyone to targets and performance reports, including comments and action plans. It was therefore decided that this information should be made available on the corporate intranet.

KMP did not feel ready to undertake a large and expensive software project for this. The company wanted to have a solution available during the first months of the year, in order to make the scorecards visible and used. Faced with a price for software products ranging from less than US$2000 to up to 100 times that sum, KMP purchased one of the cheapest products it could find, which provided little more than a customized web page with links to spreadsheets that required manual input. After toying around with this for a few weeks, an employee in the IT department built a similar but more suitable tool, and it was decided to use this instead.

This "homemade" software was seen as a temporary tool. It required managers to input measurements for their departments manually, but as much of this information came from various informal systems or from personal estimates, they would have to do this anyway. There may even be an advantage in the manual input of information, as managers have to take personal responsibility not only for inputting values but also for providing comments and suggested actions. As they do this monthly, in effect managers are publishing a report on their department's performance for everyone in the organization to see. It is also widely known that management uses these intranet pages during their regular meetings, to judge progress, and to discuss future plans.

After using this simple tool for less than a year, discussions ensued about buying some "real" software for scorecards. KMP is probably now in a better position to do this thanks to its makeshift solution. It also proved that as long as the organization tolerates – maybe even prefers – some manual tasks and can live without sophisticated links or access rules, the use of standardized tools can be both cheap and fast. However, this should probably be seen primarily as a temporary solution until scorecard use has matured, when it will be easier to specify realistic software requirements.

NOTES

1 A US consultancy founded by the originators of the balanced score-card, Kaplan and Norton.

05

The Global Dimension

The major contribution of balanced scorecards to management control is to improve communication about strategy. For a global organization this will be especially valuable, as it needs to convey the uniqueness of its offerings to more distant customers, and its business logic to employees and partners everywhere. It may also need to adapt its modes of operation to different cultures, the use of scorecards to agree on how business models can be allowed to differ. Case illustration: Oriflame.

GLOBAL COMPETITION DRIVES ARTICULATION OF STRATEGY

Increasingly, companies tell us their markets are global – or at least much larger than they used to be. Trade liberalization and the internet mean that many organizations may hope for business in countries where, traditionally, they did not have any presence. Not just geographical borders are crumbling, industry demarcations are becoming less clear-cut, and in this way, companies are gaining business from customers they have not targeted traditionally. This is also happening for quite small organizations that are trading without any physical representation near their new customers, or with just an agent or a small local branch to represent them.

Why can an organization suddenly present itself as an attractive supplier for customers outside its established markets? We believe it is because "soft" dimensions, such as experience, solutions, concepts, and contacts, are so important in today's business world. Credibility used to demand "hard" assets and facts: production plants, storerooms, and financial data showing many years of successful operation. Today, in some cases it has been enough to have a convincing business model and the ability to project it over the internet – proving a superior skill in fulfilling customers' needs. Know-how can often be transferred and applied rapidly, without building the traditional forms of presence.

The opposite side of this coin is that even organizations that decide to "stay at home", close to their traditional customers both geographically and in terms of industry, are now threatened by global competitors. Their long-term clients now realize there is a choice, and often feel that they should test alternatives. In order to keep their business, "local" organizations also have to become more skilled at presenting a convincing business case as to why they should remain the trusted supplier.

Globalization thus drives the need for organizations to develop, articulate, and present a persuasive business model – the logic according to which they build their strategies. This logic should be convincing for all the different people an organization depends on:

» customers should regard it as a reason why this business can provide better value-for-money than its competitors;

» employees and business partners should regard it as a reason to work with this business rather than another one;
» owners should regard it as a reason to invest their money; and
» society should regard it as a reason for encouraging and aiding the business.

That globalization drives uniqueness is perhaps rather natural: as markets become wider, competing alternatives will be more numerous and more differentiated. In the Western world, this development also occurs because many basic needs have already been satisfied. Business books are full of speculation about the service or knowledge economy. It is obvious that, in order to be successful, companies will increasingly depend on their ability to describe and mobilize the assets that distinguish them from their competitors. Often, these will be "soft" assets, perhaps even drawing strength from "local" qualities in a global world.

SCORECARDS AND THE GLOBAL BUSINESS

Many cases of "concepts" have been successful globally, often to the surprise of incumbent organizations in local markets. Some concepts have been made into franchises (such as McDonald's); others have remained tightly held, even family-owned businesses (such as IKEA).

How do you communicate and implement a business model like these? In most cases, the answer has been to roll it out country by country, relying on people with long experience to act as "teachers". Some may feel that this slow progress is not enough in today's world. And, teaching the model may not be the best approach. Local dialects need to be encouraged and this requires a more interactive way of determining the required parts of the strategy and what may be left to local discretion.

How can scorecards be used in this process? There are some obvious benefits from the use of scorecards.

» It is your *uniqueness* you want to convey and this often rests on some specific new concept. Customers and employees need to believe in your business logic, and scorecards are useful in describing it in a dynamic way.
» The business logic often needs to be adapted to local conditions if your organization will be building on-site presence in new markets.

Discussions about drivers and outcomes will be useful for identifying local adaptations of the corporate logic.

» In starting up in new markets, there will normally be a time lag before intended business outcomes are achieved. Watching the scorecard's performance drivers is an excellent way of monitoring if the process of building your presence in the market is on track.

CASE STUDY: ORIFLAME

Oriflame describes itself as "an expansive global cosmetics group with direct selling operations in over 60 countries. Our annual sales total €450m and close to 1,000,000 independent distributors have now joined our sales force". From its headquarters outside Brussels, a small corporate team oversees its expansion, aiming "to build the world's leading direct selling cosmetics company. We will achieve this goal by becoming the natural first choice to our customers, distributors and employees". Although Oriflame does have a number of manufacturing units worldwide, its identity comes mainly from its "soft" assets: its models for distribution and for remunerating distributors, its brand, and the qualities associated with the brand. Reaching out to almost a million people who act as part-time sellers of its products in markets as far-flung as India, Russia, and Egypt, the 3000 people who actually are employed by Oriflame face an interesting challenge in expanding its business.[1] Key elements in this are:

» frequent catalogues in a large range of languages;
» training of distributors;
  product development, including the ability to react quickly to market responses; and
» constant attention to the properties and connotations of the products and the brand.

Oriflame started its balanced scorecard project in a somewhat unusual way. Having studied the literature and experiences from other companies, a small project team at the top level asked the management in 10 different units to devise strategy maps, drawn in accordance with the scorecard format. Selected for this exercise were six national companies, representing different levels of maturity – in terms of the national economies, Oriflame experience in the market, and prior use of the balanced scorecard model. In addition, one production plant, the marketing department, and a few more units were selected. The CEO was also to draw his strategy map. All the scorecards were then presented at the annual planning conference attended by all senior managers.

Oriflame's business model is intended to be basically the same in all markets – indeed, it could be said to provide the uniqueness that is Oriflame's bid to succeed everywhere. This means that the scorecards and strategy maps for different countries could be expected to be very similar. Obviously, the emphasis given to different performance drivers varies with the stage of development of a given market, as do the target numbers for drivers and outcomes. In a similar way, functional units should reflect their role in pursuing the overall aims of the group, and the corporate scorecard should fit it all together. Most organizations would probably have let the project team devise maps and scorecards that captured the essence of the firm.

However, by letting managers in so many different units start the process by drawing their own scorecards, Oriflame achieved a number of aims:

» more widespread testing and, hopefully, acceptance for its scorecard project;
» competing ideas about how to articulate its business idea, and maybe also to adapt it to local conditions; and
» proof that it was acceptable to challenge the CEO's strategy map – in an ideas-driven company where managers share in the growth of the business over a few decades, it is important to have many of them contributing their experiences.

After the planning conference, the scorecard project continued, this time with all units involved. There is now more guidance as the "test" strategy maps and scorecards exist, and a number of corporate measures are also included in all scorecards. However, each unit is still asked to develop a strategy map of its own, "as long as the applicable parts of Oriflame's overall strategy are incorporated". There are also common definitions of measures, requirements for how to use them, and the company intends to install software to support the use of scorecards.

Oriflame provides an illustration of a company expecting to benefit from the use of scorecards and strategy maps in its endeavour to spread its business model globally. Currently, there does not seem to be any intention to use scorecards with distributors – villagers in India selling Oriflame cosmetics to their neighbors may not have a need for them! However, in many markets scorecards may be useful when explaining the Oriflame mode of operating to people who are not among its employees: government officials, local community leaders, and maybe large distributors, at least in the more developed markets. All of these will need convincing arguments as to why Oriflame can be trusted and will benefit them.

DIALECTS OF A COMMON LANGUAGE

Local dialects need to be encouraged, we said. Yet scorecards are sometimes used to control strict adherence to prescriptions from headquarters. Obviously, how dialects may be allowed to differ is a vital issue for organizations wanting to pursue globalization, and scorecards could be used to clarify this.

Some large corporations prescribe a certain number of measures but leave a certain freedom for subunits to add metrics that are relevant at their level in the organization. Similarly, a global organization should make sure that mandated measures focus on the common business model that should exist everywhere, but not include among these mandated, measures that are not relevant in cultures or business situations that are different from that of the head office.

For companies such as Oriflame, whose slogan ''natural Swedish cosmetics'' reflects its origins but which is now truly international, scorecards may be a useful vehicle for sorting out what remains constant and what should be allowed to differ between countries. This is an example of how strategy discussions facilitated by score-cards may benefit the global organization in its quest towards global identity.

NOTE

1 This network of agents can be described in terms of a "virtual" or "imaginary" organization, or an "extended enterprise". Scorecards may prove to be useful tools in providing direction and leadership in such structures.

06

The State of the Art

Successful introduction of scorecards consists of an initial stage where scorecards and the processes for their use are designed, followed by an on-going "living with scorecards" as part of organizational control, learning, and revision of strategies. This process is traced in some detail, together with examples of scorecard design (including "strategy maps"). Comment is also made on topics such as scorecards for non-profit making organizations, responsibilities for scorecards, requirements for measures, and bonus systems.

AIMS AND CRITICAL ISSUES WHEN USING SCORECARDS

Balanced scorecards provide a valuable tool for enabling employees to understand their company's situation. This understanding is vital if an organization is to achieve the dynamism it needs to be competitive in the long run. Scorecards also provide information for management, as an organization starts to develop and document on a continuous basis those measures for control that will guide it most quickly towards achieving its goals and its vision.

The use of scorecards results in daily operations being founded on a shared view of whereabouts an organization should be headed in the long term. In addition, control of operations will be perceived locally as more relevant than with previous models. Employees will understand more and be better motivated, and thus will be more open to change and being positive about implementing company decisions. The organization also becomes better at learning, is more perceptive, and continually develops its competence.

All of this, however, demands that the introduction and continued use of scorecards are performed well. As the idea of scorecards is so simple, the needs for resource commitment and top management focus are often underestimated. A scorecard project may easily be perceived as just some kind of more elaborate performance measurement project; it may even cause antagonism among employees, being seen as a new way to inspect their work. Or, initially it is well-received, but when employees receive the (sometimes correct) impression that managers are not themselves really engaged in the use of scorecards to discuss business and performance in new ways, the enthusiasm for the project evaporates.

So, how can the process be designed to avoid these dangers? In this chapter, critical issues are discussed using the following structure.

» *Developing the initial scorecards*: it is obviously of vital importance to launch the project in a good way.
» *Different ways of presenting the scorecard*: there are several different possible formats, and sometimes a combination is the best choice. Although it may seem a cosmetic issue, visual representation has a strong impact on what people perceive as "the" scorecard.

» *For what business activities should there be scorecards?* Among the first decisions to be made is where to start. The usefulness of scorecards for non-profit making activities (for example, staff units or government agencies) is also discussed.

» *Living with scorecards*: the previous sections essentially deal with the start of a scorecard project. But it is in the use of scorecards on an ongoing basis that the real gains are to be made. It is also at this stage that enthusiasm about the project is likely to diminish, as top managers believe that scorecards are safely introduced.

» *Building and using scorecards – a process view*: continuing on the previous point, the desired connection from strategy, through control and learning, back to strategy is demonstrated.

DEVELOPING THE INITIAL SCORECARDS

The initial development process consists of several steps, presented below. The final product will be a description of the business logic of the organization. This description may be made in different formats, but usually takes the form of documents and slides. There is a danger that once these physical documents have been produced, they will be seen as proof of a successful project that has reached its final destination. But this is when the real work starts, that of using the scorecard as a strategic management tool throughout the whole organization. This aspect is emphasized later in this chapter.

Preparing the project

As with any other project, careful preparations make up the foundations of a successful balanced scorecard project. The organization has to decide the scope and level of ambition of the project. Answers are needed to questions such as the following.

» *What is our level of ambition?* Initially, a project could concentrate on just a corporate scorecard, or as a pilot, focus on some subsidiary business. It could be restricted to a strategy map for general guidance, or aim for implementation as a full-blown control process.

» *What is our time schedule?* It may not be necessary to plan several years ahead, but there should be a shared view of what should be achieved during the next 12 months.

» *Who will be responsible for what?* Various competencies will be needed, and it is essential for success to include important people and groups within the organization. Will they have the time and the will to engage in this project?

» *Should we use consultants or not?* Consultants can provide experience, a fresh perspective, and work capacity to the project. On the other hand, it is important that the project is not perceived as something consultants do for us – responsibility has to rest with the internal project team.

The first step is to collect material on the characteristics and requirements of the industry and the current position and role of the organization. This starts by defining the industry, describing its development, and the role of the organization in this context. The project team (or its consultants) should do this through individual interviews with top management and with the most influential opinion leaders in the organization. By use of this method a platform for elaborating vision and future strategies is constructed.

Running the first seminar

When preparing for the first seminar it has proved useful to document initial interviews, in particular any dissenting views on essential issues. In preparation for the seminar it is also important to find out what the interviewees believe will happen in the future. This procedure involves a combination of research and interviews with stakeholders and people at different levels in the organization. At the seminar, the global picture provided by the participants is presented in summary form.

Above all, during the first seminar the vision of the organization should be confirmed or, in some cases, established. The organization will usually have had such discussions many times before.

Since the balanced scorecard model is based on a shared comprehensive vision, it is essential to ascertain at an early stage whether there really is a jointly held vision. The simple format of the scorecard triggers a concrete and realistic discussion, whereas existing strategies often comprise beautiful and non-committal words.

The next step is to choose and establish the different perspectives on which to build the scorecard. For each of these perspectives the vision has to be broken down, overall strategic aims formulated, and critical factors for success identified. This step is about articulating, refining, and agreeing on business strategy. There is an element of invention involved here that is not easily described. Given the right participants, enough time, and a discussion leader who knows how to challenge the group, it is usually an intense and fascinating process.

Confirming the top-level scorecard

When the vision, strategic aims, perspectives, and critical success factors have been established it is time to develop relevant key measures. The feasibility of taking measurements for each of them must be evaluated whilst their structure is checked for logical consistency.

The great challenge is to find clear cause and effect relationships and to create a balance between measures in different perspectives. Short-term improvements should not conflict with long-term goals. Measures in different perspectives must not encourage sub-optimization, but rather fit and support the comprehensive vision and the overall strategy of the organization.

The top-level scorecard is then put together for presentation and approval. This may be done through consultations, a second seminar, or at an ordinary meeting by the executive team. Implementation is facilitated if everyone in the organization is briefed on the work and the thinking that has gone into the scorecard. Seminar participants should receive advice about the continuing process of breaking down the scorecard: explanatory text, possible approaches, and suggestions for group work.

Roll-out

The next step is to derive lower-level scorecards from the top-level one. As employees need to see clearly how the vision and overall goals of the organization affect day-to-day operations, scorecards are needed down to a level where they become sufficiently tangible and understandable to have an impact on daily actions.

The targets for every measure have to be aligned both horizontally and vertically in order to be consistent with the comprehensive vision and overall strategy. Finally, to complete the scorecard, specific steps must be taken to achieve the goals and the vision that have been established. This action plan should include both the people responsible and a schedule for interim and final reporting.

DIFFERENT WAYS TO ILLUSTRATE THE SCORECARD

The visual representation of scorecards is vitally important during the process we just discussed. Here we will present the major ways this can be done.

Figure 6.1 shows clearly how metrics are derived. The number of levels in this analysis, and their names, differ. In most cases, for instance, vision and business idea would be just one level. Further down, there will be targets and action plans for each metric.

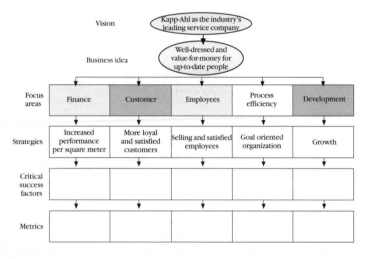

Fig. 6.1 Illustrating a scorecard vertically: KappAhl (2001).

The documentation of scorecards often takes the form of Fig. 6.2. This is similar to Fig. 6.1 but rotated through 90° as some find this more convenient. By way of illustration, some typical aims and success

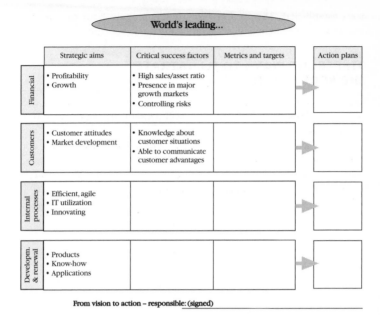

Fig. 6.2   A scorecard template for a manufacturing company.

factors have been included. During scorecard seminars, a template like this may be used to structure the discussion.

To communicate the basic logic of some activity or unit, scorecards may sometimes be summarized as in Fig. 6.3, using the original way of drawing scorecards (see Fig. 2.1). When compared to Figure 6.1 and Figure 6.2, this highlights the links between perspectives.

As mentioned in Chapter 3, "strategy maps" like the one shown in Fig. 6.4 have been found increasingly useful in articulating strategy. For variety, here is shown an example of a strategy map for a non-profit making organization. Somewhat like the internal administrative unit in Fig. 6.3, "owners" (here, the *trustees*) need to evaluate benefits and costs. The *processes* creating these cover the whole sequence, from positioning the school in its environment to assisting alumni. The

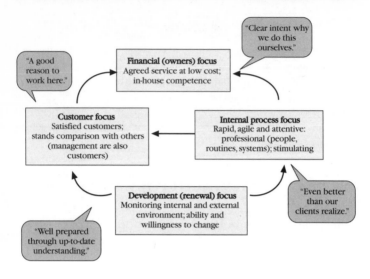

Fig. 6.3 A scorecard for an administrative unit.

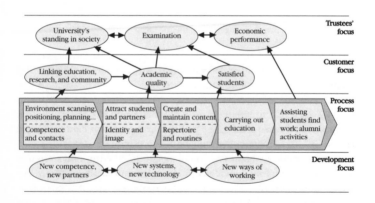

Fig. 6.4 A strategy map for a graduate school within a university – initial draft.

school may want to regard as its *customers* not just students but also its contribution to research and society. (Note that if the entire university had been included, research and society contacts would have figured more prominently in the graph.) Finally, here *development* means the changes in processes through the introduction of new competence, technology, etc. The point of using this format for illustrating the scorecard is that it highlights the need for a balance not just between perspectives when describing the school but also between activities within the perspectives.

FOR WHAT BUSINESS ACTIVITIES SHOULD THERE BE SCORECARDS?

Appropriate levels in the organization

Some organizations start their scorecard projects in the higher echelons, others with a pilot project further down the organization. Some never descend below the higher levels of the organization, whereas others even develop scorecards for individual employees. A decision is clearly needed about which activities should be covered by scorecards.

The dialog used on the scorecards also needs to be determined. A departmental scorecard could be used entirely for internal purposes (motivating employees, for example). It would normally also be used to agree with, and report on, performance to higher levels of management. It might also be published on a corporate intranet as part of a description of the department.

The unit chosen for the initial scorecard needs to be fairly complete and self-contained, or should have a clear task and vision assigned by its owners. Otherwise the attempt to develop a scorecard will only result in a lot of questions about its vision and logic. Even this may be useful – some scorecard projects result in a ''proposal'' from a subsidiary to corporate management about the role it wants. There are also practical matters involved: how large a part of the total organization will it be feasible and cost-efficient to include?

Extending scorecard work down to individual employees has proved useful when their tasks are more independent; otherwise teams would be the normal level at which to stop. How useful this will be also depends on a number of factors, such as the improvements aimed for in the project, links to development talks, and effects on remuneration.

Usefulness for support ("non-profit") functions within organizations

Scorecards are very useful for discussing the internal support functions that provide the infrastructure in most organizations, in order to:

» justify the extent and expense of such functions, by articulating the links to expected benefits and their impact on profits;
» prioritize the demands of various users of such services; and
» boost the morale of employees in support functions, by showing how their efforts contribute to business success for the entire organization.

The most common use of scorecards in this way has been for information technology (IT) and human resources (HR) functions and departments. The customer perspective describes service-level agreements. As in any scorecard, internal processes and development should be described as separate perspectives. In this way, management will receive a full description of the IT or HR "business" which forms part of the organization. This will be especially useful when comparing it with the alternative of outsourcing activities. IT outsourcing sometimes turns out to be only a short-term success because the decision to outsource was based only on current service deliveries, not the process and development assets which disappeared with outsourcing. This situation could be avoided with a scorecard that provides a more complete picture of the IT department.

It will sometimes be useful to discuss internal services as departments and as functions separately. An IT or HR *department* may be considered as just said: as a "business" serving internal customers. Like any business it needs to take care of its assets and develop over time. The IT or HR *function* includes activities by all employees. A scorecard for this will show how the organization uses and develops its IT or HR resources, and this task will extend far beyond the walls of the corresponding departments.

A department scorecard is illustrated in Figure 6.3 above. The unit shown in this figure might include some of the following when discussing this scorecard.

» *Owners*: clearly, this unit is not making a profit by itself. Is it mean-ingful to discuss its cost–benefit ratio by evaluating its contribution to business success? Are there external alternatives (shared services; outsourcing)? Is management just interested in adequate services at the lowest possible cost, or does the unit perform some staff function that has value for owners and management?

» *Customers*: these will usually be the employees, but just like a government agency, there will be "services" provided that customers do not ask for: a requirement to fill in expense reports, for example. Employees rarely pay for administrative services and may make unrealistic demands on them. If the administrative unit contributes to good working conditions, it may have indirect effects on productivity and employee turnover.

» *Internal processes*: top management should recognize that the "structural capital" contained in established procedures and the latest improvements in the function may not yet have had their full impact on its customers or costs.

» *Development*: any operation should have sufficient time to import new ideas and technology from outside, or develop them itself. The ability to renew itself may determine whether the tasks of an administrative unit, long-term, should be performed in-house or outsourced.

Use in government and other non-profit making organizations

Profit-seeking organizations use scorecards to clarify links between current activities and long-term profits. In non-profit making orga-nizations there rarely is any such long-term, single goal. Instead, scorecards have an important role in facilitating discussions about trade-offs between diverse interests, and the general level of ambition within a specific policy area. This is similar to the internal services discussed above.

Scorecards have been introduced in central and local government organizations in several countries. For instance, the Swedish Associ-ation of Local Authorities has organized training classes for balanced scorecard "coaches". It seems that the more successful cases so far are found at lower levels in such organizations, where scorecards provide ordinary employees with an opportunity to clarify roles and expectations, and to present their view of "business logic" to their superiors. For instance, in some parts of Sweden the police departments use scorecards for town and patrol levels of their organization, deciding priorities between different kinds of actions and police duties.

On the other hand, so far, the Swedish police have not introduced scorecards at a national level. Explicating the links between resource use, criminality, and public safety may be too complicated – indeed, a matter for research. However, strategies for the police will always reflect some hypotheses about these connections, and – similar to the previous discussion about service departments in companies – scorecards could help:

» to decide how extensive and expensive activities are needed, by articulating expected benefits and, ultimately, their impact on social well-being;
» to prioritize the demands and needs of various groups of citizens; and
» to boost the morale of employees by showing how their efforts contribute to society.

The four perspectives in the scorecard will need to be reinterpreted somewhat in the case of government or other non-profit making organizations. It is useful to retain the four perspectives, reinterpreting each in the following way (cf. Fig. 6.4 above).

» *Financial perspective*: an owner or "principal" perspective, showing the ultimate contribution to the needs addressed by the organization (for example, fight crime or poverty, or take custody of national art treasures).
» *Customer perspective*: an "external" perspective, describing how successful the organization is in reaching and interacting with all its contacts in society. In addition to serving customers, like a company, many organizations interact with less willing clients, such as criminals who are the targets of police actions. Their experiences should be part of the scorecard, but not by itself an objective.
» *Process perspective* and *development perspective*: no major changes, as the internal processes of all organizations should be efficient and

managed well. Just like in any scorecard, the principals of a non-profit making organization should take an interest in how its "process capital" is maintained and utilized. Likewise, non-profit making organizations will need to import and implement new technology and new skills.

Non-governmental, non-profit making organizations also include charities and voluntary organizations. Some of these also have found it useful to agree on a "business logic" that can be used for motivating donors and employees alike in supporting their activities.

LIVING WITH SCORECARDS

Some companies developed an initial set of scorecards but never managed to make them part of an ongoing, living process. Here, we discuss what is needed to achieve this.

Management control or merely performance measurement?

In order to get beyond just measuring and reporting, scorecards must be seen as a way of communicating achievements and comparing them to commitments. Scorecards have sometimes been introduced as a substitute for budgeting, which has been described as a rigid, antiquated, and bureaucratic form of management control. But there is an obvious danger that scorecard metrics will be perceived as similarly rigid and bureaucratic – a new and more detailed form of supervision!

For scorecards to be meaningful, constant discussion of their underlying logic is essential. When employees perceive the metrics as a more extended set of standards, all the negative effects of traditional supervision may occur. But, if similar metrics are perceived as part of a living dialog about what is worth doing, and how performance relates to organizational progress, they have often been welcomed. Achieving this requires management to be able to engage in such dialogs – to have enough knowledge about their business and a viewpoint about its possible futures.

Because of this, scorecards will be most useful at the business unit level and lower down in corporations. Here, management should have this knowledge. Near the top, control often is mostly financial – except where an organization tries to pursue synergies that require a more detailed grasp of business-unit performance.

The exact mixture of traditional budgets, scorecards, and forecasts will be a consequence of several things: the organization's tradition and strategies, its competitive situation, industry conditions, and the level within the organization. Business units pursuing differentiation from the competition through long-term activities will have the greatest need for scorecards.

Responsibilities for scorecards

In order to get a scorecard project going, responsibilities need to be assigned. These should cover a variety of aspects of "living with scorecards". Obviously, every manager whose unit is part of the new control system is accountable for proper attention to its scorecard. The "technology" of scorecards (definitions, formats, timetable, information provision) needs to be the responsibility of someone, usually in the controller's department. During the first year or two, this may also include promoting and training for scorecard use; responsibility for this is given to a special task force near top management. If software is introduced, someone, usually in the IT department, will be accountable for it's functioning. As data is collected about the various metrics, someone should periodically assess this in order to learn about cause and effect relationships. Did the patterns play out as expected, or should the links in strategic maps be reconsidered?

Requirements for measures

By introducing scorecards and designing them in a particular way, management direct attention to issues that it deems important, and the logic inherent in a scorecard reinforces a strategic perspective. This requires a number of things.

1 That measures are chosen that reflect the strategic aims of the activities that they portray (*relevant and logical scorecards*).
2 That measurements may be taken with valid and credible methods (*accepted and practical*).
3 That a reporting format is designed which will bring scorecards to the attention of people who should take an interest and react (*available and accessible*).

4 That scorecards are accompanied with analysis and action plans that reflect what actions will be taken based on the data and the status of any previously announced actions (*actionable*).

5 That there are incentives to take an interest in the scorecards and use them as a basis for action (*perceived as important*). This is also influenced through other control practices and the way higher management, in general, signals priorities.

6 That there is feedback and a constant urge to use the scorecard to accumulate experience, refine the business logic on which it is based, and modify the scorecard over time (*useful for learning*).

It is practical to use similar measures throughout an organization to describe a particular phenomenon. Organizations that wish to follow customer satisfaction or time to customer for all their units will normally require the same measures to be used everywhere. This carries the danger that the set of metrics, mandated from the top, will be perceived as just a part of corporate control, and not an invitation to discuss local strategic realities. Many organizations also leave room for a number of locally selected metrics, and encourage local units to develop and present their own strategy maps in order to gain involvement.

In connection with reward systems, scorecard metrics are sometimes combined into a single index of success. This may also encourage the use of similar metrics throughout.

IT support

A scorecard project will find it easier to "take root" if measurements are "available and accessible", as pointed out above. This is partly a matter of information systems, and readers are referred to Chapter 4 for views on this. The preference is for starting in a quick and simple way, even if this requires some manual work. In the longer run, most organizations benefit from having scorecard information readily available over an intranet.

Will scorecards have any impact without new reward systems?

We have not observed any scorecard project where changes in formal compensation were part of the original design. Many projects arrived at this issue slowly and reluctantly, probably because large financial incentives were rare in Scandinavian companies until recently. Traditional values do not encourage them, and a highly unionized workforce has stressed other priorities in its wage negotiations.

For some time after the introduction of scorecards, the attention paid to the "new" measures may encourage performance improvements – especially among employees who were involved in setting targets. For a more lasting impact, non-financial measures must be made "competitive" with the financial and traditionally more visible ones.

In order to calculate financial rewards, most organizations weight scorecard measures, or simply link them to some of the measures. Designers of scorecard software often include combined scores, indicated by speedometer-like symbols or green, yellow, and red traffic lights. This has to be done with great care, if at all. Combining numbers into a single index replaces the balance of a scorecard with a fixed relationship between measures, making it less natural to discuss and learn about. It also invites opportunistic behavior, where people concentrate on measures that carry high weights and rewards compared to the efforts required.

If a bonus system is desired – and sometimes it may be valuable – design it as a sequence of requirements. For instance, achieving a necessary level of profits may be a "must" if any bonus is to be awarded, whereas exceeding this level should not be encouraged. Instead, additional bonuses may be linked to attracting new customers, or introducing new technologies, as long as minimum levels for *all* metrics are reached. To win even higher bonuses, managers may need to improve employee motivation, for example.

Building and using scorecards – a process view

In many early balanced scorecard texts and projects, there was understandable emphasis on the construction of an initial set of scorecards. "Living with scorecards" therefore received too little attention. On the other hand, administrators of scorecard projects sometimes overemphasize software support and reporting formats, forgetting that strategy has to be the starting point. Figure 6.5 shows that both are needed in order to create management control systems for a learning organization.

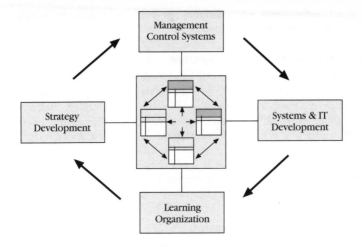

Fig. 6.5 The balanced scorecard process.

Strategy development

It has been emphasized that scorecards are tools for controlling a business, and realizing an organization's vision and strategy. However, developing scorecards usually makes people see their organization and its business model in a new way. This often leads to new ideas about the vision of the organization, and to a reconsideration of its strategy. For this reason the first steps in the scorecard process are about developing or confirming a strategy.

Management control systems

The process presented in this chapter emphasizes strongly how organizational strategies are translated into measures and goals for various managers and how the scorecard provides comprehensive, balanced statements of their duties. In principle, the process should be repeated at every level so that all employees are given a sense of participation and can understand their part in the overall strategic scheme of the organization. An important part of the process, therefore, is to link together measures in different perspectives and in scorecards for different business units.

IT and systems development

For the scorecard to be usable in practice throughout the organization, the procedure for handling measurements must be user-friendly and not overly complicated. Data must be recorded, verified, and made available. Normally the scorecard will draw on a combination of data already in use within the organization, and of new measurements, some of which may be quite informal in nature. Sometimes data will be imported from outside sources, such as market surveys or competitor benchmarking. To create interest and high attention throughout the organization is often an essential part of a scorecard project.

The learning organization

The primary function of the scorecard is to control the organization's operations. It furnishes a language for describing expectations and performance, thus laying the foundation for discussions on how each individual can contribute to fulfilling the organization's vision.

By extension, there is also a more cumulative effect. As experience is gained in how a new customer database is being used, or how sales are developing in new customer segments, assumptions about causal relationships will be confirmed or disproved. In this way the use of the balanced scorecard may also facilitate learning. At both individual and organizational levels, a better understanding of the relationship between what we do and how well the business succeeds may be developed.

07

In Practice

Short case studies from a variety of firms and countries: KappAhl, a Scandinavian retailer; Ericsson Enterprise, part of a Swedish-based multinational; Ricoh and Xerox, two Japanese and US multinationals in largely the same industry; and ATOM Transportation, a Japanese company. Examples of their scorecards are shown, but the emphasis is on their different approaches in using scorecards and their differing degrees of success.

The cases in this chapter illustrate different experiences with score-cards, and different ambitions for their use. They are not all exemplary: indeed, one is almost a cautionary tale. But all provide learning opportunities for those wishing to design a balanced-scorecard project adapted to the needs and conditions of their organization.

» KappAhl, a Swedish company which embarked on its scorecard project in 1995 and where it has become a key element in control.
» Ericsson Enterprise, part of a Swedish-based multinational, which has taken a highly decentralized approach to the use of scorecards.
» Ricoh, a Japanese corporation that – in contrast – uses scorecards to communicate strategies from the top.
» Xerox, a US multinational whose quality projects were unified into a common scorecard for all units, but found this less helpful when the company faced a crisis.
» ATOM Transportation, a smaller Japanese company with similar tasks performed in different regions, where scorecards are seen as a path towards independent teams being guided by rewards based on scorecards.

Books and articles have reported business successes related to the use of scorecards. The first among our cases below is one example. However, we have not seen any systematic evaluation, and it is doubtful that one would be possible. As already argued, the possible uses of scorecards, how they are combined with other controls, and the ''dialects'' in adapting scorecards to the particular situation, are simply too many to associate such success in any certain way with the introduction of scorecards.

KAPPAHL – SUSTAINED USE OF SCORECARDS[1]

The KappAhl retail clothing chain was started in 1954 and became one of Sweden's greatest success stories of the 1950s and 1960s. By 1990, when the company had grown quite large it was acquired by KF, the Swedish Co-operative Wholesale Society. However, for the time being, the days of glory were over, and despite a succession of management changes, it proved difficult to restore profitability.

In the mid-1990s KappAhl had 150 stores and 2000 employees in Sweden, Norway, and Finland. With sales of more than SKr2bn and a market share of nearly five per cent, the company was one of the largest specialized retail trade chains in the Nordic countries. But losses grew worse, amounting to almost SKr150mn in 1995. In the fall of that year, a new chief executive officer (CEO) was appointed. The new management reorganized the company, cut staff by 25%, and renamed the Gothenburg headquarters the "service office." But more was needed.

In connection with the restructuring, a process to develop scorecards for KappAhl was initiated in the winter of 1995/96. Two consultants retained to interview various people at the company conducted a small survey, primarily to find out what was on the minds of employees. Their work led to the first of several seminars, where the KappAhl vision would be established. A total of 25 people took part, including a new and enlarged top management team.

Although the discussions remained on a very general level, a consensus began to emerge that KappAhl had gone too far in imitating the efforts of competitors to focus on a youthful target group. KappAhl's strength and "soul" was to be found in another profile – that of a service company for the general public, but with an up to date image.

After the summer of 1996, the vision, mission statement, and main strategies were revised and confirmed. Management appointed a project group with the task of continuing the balanced scorecard process. During the 1996 fall the project group worked at the different steps in developing a top-level scorecard. The resulting scorecard was then reviewed and adjusted after being presented to the larger group from the seminar. The KappAhl scorecard at this time included the usual four perspectives, for each of which the following strategic goals were formulated.

» *Finance*: profit and cash flow.
» *Customer*: customer satisfaction.
» *Process*: workflow approach and small-scale operation.
» *Development*: being one step ahead.

The thinking of the project group led to the presentation of a top-level scorecard for KappAhl before the 25 seminar participants; the scorecard had been developed to include success factors, measures, and goals. However, action plans were deliberately avoided at this point;

these were to be prepared by the responsible units once management had approved the top-level scorecard.

This documentation was turned over to 15 different project groups corresponding to units in the formal organization. The groups were asked to prepare scorecards for their respective units at KappAhl; each unit was to determine how it could contribute to achieving the vision in the top-level scorecard.

KappAhl proceeded with the subsequent steps in the various units of the company – that is, of the service office – before extending the process six months later to the numerous stores of the organization. Since conditions in the different stores are fairly similar, the company decided to let one store in each of the three countries first prepare a test scorecard that would be submitted to the project group for evaluation. For this reason most stores were not involved in the process until the 1997 fall, more that two years after it had begun.

The project group maintained continuous contact with the 15 different units as they were developing their scorecards, both to pass experience along and to see that the project maintained momentum and remained consistent with the purposes indicated in the KappAhl top-level scorecard. The decision was made to give the groups written feedback. It was important to make sure that the measures were well defined and that goals were set at reasonable levels, and that there were no potential conflicts between the different goals.

Interestingly enough, after a time KappAhl decided to add a fifth, employee perspective to the four usual ones. In the form of a combined value chain and causal analysis, the company also attempted to show how measures for different parts of the organization are related to the business of the company as a whole.

KappAhl did not begin to introduce more formal reporting procedures until it extended the scorecard process to the stores during the winter of 1997/98. At the service office it had been easy for everyone to adopt the new ideas. True, expectations were not overly high – the concept of a scorecard was unknown, and management tended to be sceptical after having worked with total quality management (TQM) and a number of other recipes for change. However, in the new situation, with new management and the company facing an acute crisis, everyone readily accepted this way of thinking, and even without any formal system of performance monitoring, the scorecards for the different units at KappAhl proved to be a major factor in turning the company around. This undertaking was extremely successful; the company was already showing a profit exceeding SKr100mn in 1997.

The managing director deserves much of the credit for the importance given to the scorecard development process. His actions and those of the scorecard project group that represented him made the process highly visible. It was also significant that the project group consisted of people who, by virtue of their position and personality, demonstrated the priority of the project. It may be noted that accounting staff were present but did not dominate the process; the project manager himself, for example, was not an accountant.

Today the KappAhl balanced scorecard functions as the common language. The company succeeded in the difficult process of moving from initial implementation to a situation where the scorecard became widely accepted and used as its main strategic tool. However, the scorecard is not being used as a replacement for the traditional budgeting and market planning processes, but rather as a co-ordinating tool for the overall strategic business control.

The top-level scorecard is revised and adjusted once every year. It is based on the strategic priorities established by the company's board and executive management. The contents of the scorecard may seem rather traditional, containing several metrics that are not unique in any way. Over the years it has gradually become more focused and specific, in order to clarify business strategies and the overall message. Measures that proved too generic, such as customer and employee satisfaction, have been given more precise meaning. KappAhl now aims for "more satisfied *and loyal* customers" and "*selling* and satisfied employees". This adds another dimension to the expression "satisfaction" which was used earlier, and illustrates how satisfied customers and employees are directly related to the overall financial performance of the company. The KappAhl top-level scorecard was presented earlier in Figure 6.1.

KappAhl has also learned that it is important to concentrate on a few, short-term, key issues at a time. This is why the strategic goal for the process perspective is "a goal-oriented organization".

This short-term focus has proven useful in later years when KappAhl had difficulties in attaining financial goals and consequently had to concentrate on short-term profitability. In such a situation there is an obvious risk that the financial perspective will overshadow the other perspectives, and that ongoing discussions about vision and strategy will be lost in the process. In order to handle this problem a separate top-level scorecard is produced yearly, to stress the short-term priorities and goals and focus on profitability. But, since all perspectives are included, the risk of overlooking the big picture is significantly reduced.

At lower levels in the organization, the respective units prepare their own scorecards. These scorecards are also rather traditional and explain how each unit can have an impact on critical success factors. They contain action plans that describe in concrete terms how units can contribute to achieving the vision in the top-level scorecard. An illustration of how such an action plan may be derived from critical success factors and measures is presented in Fig. 7.1.

Follow-up of both the top-level and lower-level scorecards is a continuous process where they serve as the agenda for business control in the different units. Even though these are developed separately, the corporate controller supervises this process in order to secure that the financial reporting is co-ordinated internally and based on the information provided in the scorecards.

Another factor contributing to the success of keeping the KappAhl balanced scorecard alive, and accepted throughout the organization, has been the initial weight put on explaining the purpose and logic of the tool. Much time has been saved later in the process by dedicating resources and time at the outset to discuss the ideas and involve people at an early stage.

Since so many of the tasks within KappAhl are being performed in a balanced-scorecard context, the understanding of cause and effect relationships and the overall business model has grown significantly. The scorecard has therefore contributed to the creation of a common language that unites the company in different ways. To create this language, with key phrases and symbols that are accepted by all staff, takes a long time. In the case of KappAhl it took at least two years before the central concepts became widely accepted.

Focus:
Customer

Strategic aim:
More loyal and satisfied customers

Critical success factors:
1. Expression in shop
2. Active salespeople in every shop
3. Visitors in shop

Measures:
1. Customer per visit
2. Winning the company contest (customer contacts)
3. Number of visitors per year

Action plan:

Action	Responsible	Deadline	Done
1. Simulate shopping round at second visit in shop • Action a • Action b • Action c	Coach	March	✓
2. Market the concept for a good start • Action a • Action b	NN	April	
3. VIP customer day twice a year • Action a • Action b	Coach	April October	

Fig. 7.1 An action plan for the customer focus at KappAhl.

ERICSSON ENTERPRISE – CREATING A LANGUAGE FOR AGREEMENTS AND RESPONSIBILITIES[2]

Enterprise is the business unit within Ericsson, the Swedish-based telecom corporation, which is responsible for sales to enterprises. It has a turnover of SKr11bn. Enterprise is one of many Ericsson units using scorecards. Group level management has encouraged the use of scorecards, but there is no uniform format or group scorecard. A degree of similarity comes from the fact that almost all use the "Cockpit Communicator," which is presentation software developed by Ericsson. For an illustration of how this software is being used in Enterprise, see Fig. 4.1.

Scorecards for different units can also be accessed via the Ericsson intranet, which should encourage convergence of the measures used. At this time, however, a quick survey shows that scorecards differ substantially: in the number of perspectives and measures, and in specific metrics. Ericsson Enterprise (EE) started using scorecards in January 1999 and they have become highly accepted as a language for agreements and responsibilities. Before scorecards were introduced, there were no accepted non-financial measures. The scorecards for units within EE include both commonly defined measures and some selected by each unit. Together with rolling forecasts they provide the targets for each unit.

The use of scorecards is the key element in what EE calls performance management processes. Every month measurements are published on the intranet for every one of the 2300 employees to see. For each key performance indicator there should be two or three lines of comments about actions, and the internal board of EE follows this information closely. Starting in 2000, performance also had an impact on bonuses for managers.

Ericsson also has introduced a "self-assessment of planning and review processes", whereby managers taking part grade their success in developing adequate measures and using information. Through this process, they have identified an agenda for further improvements. These include improved cause and effect descriptions (EE had not used strategy maps until now), improved discipline in reporting, and scorecards for processes and not only for hierarchical units. The final point seems especially important as EE outsources more and more of its production and sales, to concentrate on three processes: building partner relations, managing supply chains, and product provisioning.

These developments are entirely conducted within EE, as the organization so far has had few concrete suggestions for scorecard developments within Ericsson. Given business conditions, the focus in the early 2000s was on cash generation and short-term profitability. Scorecards had established themselves as a necessary control tool within EE and were useful even with this focus.

RICOH – COMMUNICATING STRATEGY[3]

Ricoh Co., Ltd. manufactures and sells copying machines and other information-processing products such as digital cameras. The organization was founded in 1936 and is headquartered in Tokyo, Japan. In 2000, its net sales were ¥755bn (about US$6.5bn) and its number of employees more than 12,000.

Ricoh introduced scorecards for its 51 business units in October 1999. The intention then was to create a management system emphasizing strategy implementation, as the lack of growth in the Japanese economy made it crucial to focus the organization on the medium-term strategies that had been determined. That Ricoh received the Japanese Quality Award in 1999 helped greatly in its introduction of scorecards.

As shown in Fig. 7.2, Ricoh has introduced two particular features in its scorecard. One is the addition of a fifth perspective: safeguarding the environment. Another is a clear distinction between lead and lag indicators. These correspond to the performance drivers and outcome measures mentioned in Chapter 8.

Each business unit is evaluated every six months. A committee consisting of seven senior managers, including the president of Ricoh, examines performance on the lag indicators, and their evaluation has a direct impact on the bonus for the heads of the business units.

According to Ricoh, the introduction of balanced scorecards had the following consequences.

» All business units achieved their strategies.
» Relations between top management and business units were improved.
» Ricoh's president came to a better understanding of the business logic of each business unit.
» Top management understood the stage of development for each unit, and strategic imperatives for all businesses.

After using scorecards for 18 months, the process developed further. By combining it with an emphasis on management by objectives, it is expected that strategy implementation will be strengthened even more.

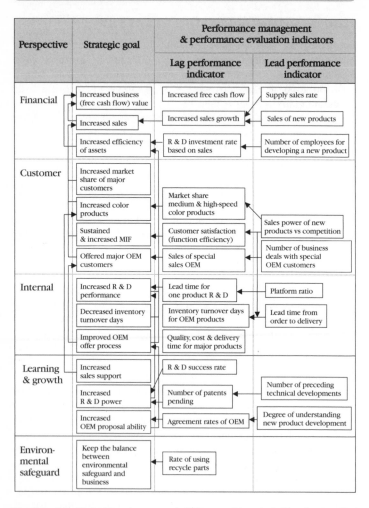

Fig. 7.2 Ricoh's balanced scorecard. MIF = machines in field = the installed base of machines; OEM = other equipment manufacturing = Ricoh producing for other brands.

XEROX – THE DANGER OF OVER-COMPLEXITY[4]

Xerox has been one of the fastest-growing American companies of the post-war era. The business of much of the company is based on the xerography principle, that is, of making copies on ordinary paper.

In the early years Xerox had a monopoly position that enabled it to achieve a return on assets (ROA) of 25–30%. At the end of the 1970s, however, its patent expired. The Japanese entered the market, and in 1979, introduced their first xerography-based photocopier on the American market. Because of its market position Xerox at first did not consider the Japanese products to be a major threat, but it soon found out that the Japanese products were being sold at a price equal to Xerox's production costs. Furthermore, the Japanese products were of superior quality. Consequently, the ROA curve dipped sharply, plummeting to a low of four per cent in 1983.

In the 1960s Xerox made the fortunate move of acquiring 50% of the Japanese company, Fuji Xerox, which in 1980 received Japan's highest citation for quality, the Deming Award. From 1979 through 1983, when Xerox was in the depths of its slump, management tried to launch the expression "leadership for quality." Xerox then "benchmarked" itself against Fuji Xerox and was subsequently able to raise profitability to a level of 18%. Not only did ROA improve, the organization's efforts were crowned with the Malcolm Baldrige Award (1989) and the European Foundation for Quality Management (EFQM) Award of 1992. To achieve this success, groups consisting of participants from all over the world were appointed to develop strategic guidelines for Xerox.

In 1990 Rank Xerox conducted a comprehensive review of its efforts to meet high standards of quality. This work resulted in a management model drawing on the ideas of Baldrige, Deming, Xerox's own work, the International Standardization Organization (ISO), and EFQM. The model helped top management to focus on a total of 42 specific measures. The model was further developed and named the Xerox Management Model (XMM). XMM focused on 31 specific measures in six different categories. Since the model had the same format all over the world, it was possible to benchmark the different units, thus simplifying learning and development. The model also provided a framework when the unit is certified once a year. In addition, the measures and categories were reviewed and published every quarter in a self-assessment portfolio.

The XMM process was pursued very systematically for some years. Although all 31 metrics were measured, it turned out that corporate management focused on only four or five. Looking back, there was a danger of over-complexity even with this small number. Many of the metrics required judgements, and senior people from Xerox subsidiaries were assigned to act as outside corporate assessors. They would visit other Xerox units and grade performance on each metric on a scale from one to seven. A major effort was then made to have corporate management discuss this information during two-day sessions. But the assessors were not as harshly realistic as they should have been. When things were presented as improvements, which top managers knew were not, they came to regard the XMM process as a waste of time. As control officially was through a matrix organization, it also turned out to be hugely difficult to devise metrics that portrayed the responsibilities in an understandable way.

Then Xerox was hit by a new competitive situation in the late 1990s, and made some mistakes in reorganizing its sales force and customer administration at the same time. Focus became much more short-term (survival). Most of the XMM structure was dismantled. Measures were still used for more operational purposes, such as print volumes and stock turns – and of course financials. But corporate management focused on just a few metrics, essentially cash generation and the balance sheet.

In the new situation, it was realized that the scorecards used previously were too generic. Business needs to be conducted in different ways in different countries, and when the current difficulties have been conquered, it is likely that top management will focus sources of differentiation, unique competencies, partnerships, etc. – making key success factors more varied across the organization. In the longer run, just having key performance indicators relating to cash flow will not be enough.

The mode of control that is now emerging will be less complex and more focused, with more stress on follow-through. Management processes need to be disciplined and structured. It is essential that people understand them and expect them to be acted on.

The Xerox experience shows that an elaborate technique for scorecard measurements does not guarantee success. The problems hitting the company may partly explain why the XMM process was abandoned, but it also was applied in a way that is now talked about as bureaucratic and too complex. On the surface, Xerox seems to have applied it diligently and systematically. But apparently it did not lead to strong commitments or enough action.

An interesting observation is that Xerox was successful in using metrics over a very long period through benchmarking between countries and units, and creating challenges for managers. When top management needed to take a more differentiated approach, and create changes that require corporate management to act forcefully, XMM turned out to be of limited use.

What does this tell us about the use of scorecards? – As we have seen XMM originated as a quality control project. Such models carry the temptation to use large numbers of metrics, and try to create, monitor and compare "complete" descriptions of performance. As proponents of scorecards, we suspect that scorecards and maybe strategy maps really describing sources of uniqueness in Xerox might have worked better – and may do so in the future. But of course we cannot know this. At least the story cautions us not to confuse an impressive façade with good management control!

ATOM TRANSPORTATION – LINKING REWARDS TO PERFORMANCE[5]

Distribution of Coca-Cola products and maintenance of its vending machines in Japan is handled by ATOM Transportation Co., Ltd. The company was founded in 1971. Last year's sales were ¥6bn (US$50mn).

ATOM introduced scorecards in 1999, in order to communicate their mission, strategies, and initiatives throughout the organization. There is a special emphasis on aligning personal goals to the mission through linking rewards to performance. The use of scorecards has led to:

» focus shifting from only financial goals, to include also non-financial ones;
» top management and heads of branches having a better understanding of their business, making it easier to resolve problems quickly; and
» the organization's mission and goals can be clarified down to truck drivers.

ATOM is still in the process of refining its scorecard programme. Scorecards will now replace budgets. The final point above has not yet been reached, but scorecards will now be developed for all 860 employees. There are even plans to change the current branch organization and run the company based on teams of five to seven people, using scorecards to create direction and motivation.

The ATOM scorecard is shown in Fig. 7.3.

Focus: Customer	Operation	Development of employee capabilities	Financial (performance)
• Market share (%) • Acquisitions (%) • Customer satisfaction • Suggestions (#) • Customer information collection (#)	• Productivity/truck • Productivity/employee • Employee turnover • Lead time of delivery • Productivity improvement • Safe driving • Truck maintenance • Accidents	• Goodwill utilization • Claims/employee • Suggestions/employee to improve working conditions • Customer questionnaire • Attendance at training • Ability to develop new employees • Spot check evalutation	• Sales • Profits

Fig. 7.3 The ATOM scorecard.

THE ''MARKET SHARE'' AND SUCCESS OF SCORECARDS

No comprehensive studies of the spread and success of scorecards are known to us. Questionnaire studies in Sweden indicate that 30–40 per cent of municipalities and manufacturing firms use some form of scorecards. It is doubtful, however, if their use of scorecards corresponds to the models provided in books like the present one.

As already stated, the use of scorecards can mean different things. For example, organizations whose systematic use of financial and non-financial metrics to create strategic focus could easily be claimed to be an example of balanced scorecards, but which choose not to call it that. Conversely, there are organizations that are happy to show their ''scorecards'', but among which a cursory study will turn up evidence that these do not really have any importance in running the company. The impression is that the huge interest in balanced scorecards shown by book sales, conferences, and consultancy assignments is gradually having a strong influence on management control practices. Most of the advice provided in this book is not linked specifically to some exact format for scorecards, and the brief cases reported here indicate a range of possibilities. Maybe in the longer run much of what has been learned from the use of scorecards will be integrated into general "best practice" in management control. Most organizations will adapt their own scorecards and strategy maps, and no longer consider this as a special type of control, and even less as a separate project.

For similar reasons, it is difficult to prove the impact of scorecard use on business results. Some case studies link the introduction of scorecards to increased profits, such as the KappAhl case above. However, scorecards will normally be part of a larger turn-around effort, and linked to the advent of a new CEO, changes in strategy, etc. Lacking the scientist's controlled experiments, we have to rely on the impressions of managers who have used balanced scorecards. Those interviewed fall into two camps.

There are the enthusiasts, like the management of KappAhl, who adopted scorecards as a format for a range of discussions in their companies. They have extended their use of scorecards patiently over a number of years. Many of them seem not to have been in any hurry to acquire any advanced software tools, but most recognize the importance of these once the scorecard process is well under way.

The other group comprises managers who feel that their efforts to introduce scorecards have failed, or proved less useful. Scorecard use was discontinued, petered out, or turned into a resource-consuming bureaucratic exercise. Some of these managers claim that the initial discussions (called "developing the initial scorecards" in Chapter 6) were useful, but that repeating this exercise within a few years will reveal most of the potential benefits from scorecards. In between, they find traditional controls sufficient, pointing to the costs of measuring and reporting new metrics. They sometimes also claim that in their business, the emphasis has to be financial, and that scorecards provide excuses for managers rather than improved focus.

When discussing these views, the reader is referred to Figure 2.2 and what was said at the end of Chapter 3. The *mix* of controls needs to be adapted to a particular situation. Frustrated attempts to introduce scorecards may reflect situations where they were less needed, but also misguided efforts to do too much, usually measuring too many things, too often, and with too high ambitions to have too many people discuss all these measurements. It is very hard to provide advice about the "right" level of effort and the "right" pace of development.

Comparing the cases reported here, KappAhl obviously provides an example where management perceived a need to communicate strategy throughout the organization. More than most companies of a similar size, a retailer is dispersed both functionally and geographically. The buying department, for instance, or a KappAhl shop that is the only one in its town, needs constantly to be reminded of the uniqueness KappAhl strives for. In the turn-around phase, when scorecards are first introduced, and again in the more austere business climate of the last few years, especially, cost reductions have to be guided by awareness of strategic priorities. It is striking how KappAhl links everyday actions to the scorecard metrics.

Xerox, although a much larger corporation, seems to have had similar needs during its problematic years: to develop a shared strategic identity. The organization may have been too ambitious in creating a process (XMM) that aimed to combine all the best features of the quality movement, and now believes that the resulting model was too generic. It did not portray the uniqueness of Xerox sufficiently. Referring once again to Figure 2.2, a large corporation such as Xerox will have to "layer" strategic control in an appropriate manner. The more detailed metrics should not be brought up to group management. A scorecard at the corporate level should focus on *corporate* success factors – attempts to control all *business* strategies are probably doomed to fail.

This may be why Ericsson as a group encourages scorecards but has not so far introduced any group scorecard or common format for business scorecards. We looked at one unit, Ericsson Enterprise, which has been building its scorecard process over the last few years and is still refining it. Important issues concerning how to use scorecards have emerged gradually – for instance, should scorecards apply to processes or just traditional responsibility centres?

Another organization still developing its use of scorecards is Ricoh. Quite apart from being in the same industry as Xerox, Ricoh seems to face the same dangers of over-complexity, as its scorecard use seems to be built around frequent and highly formal reviews. There will, of course, be many differences in culture and management style, and the Ricoh scorecards are probably more customized than the Xerox XMM model. Ricoh management stresses its improved understanding of the conditions and business logics for the various units – it seems to be more of a dialog.

The remaining case in this chapter (ATOM), and Oriflame in Chapter 5, both show earlier stages in scorecard introduction. Oriflame in particular represents an interesting attempt to involve many parts of a widespread organization at an early stage in the scorecard process in articulating a common business logic through the use of strategy maps.

Rather than summarize any findings from these cases, the reader is referred to Chapter 6 and Chapter 10, where an attempt has been made to integrate many of the things that can be learned from them.

NOTES

1 The material for this case was provided by KappAhl through Jan Roy, Concours Cepro.
2 This information was provided by Sten Olsson, manager for management systems, at Ericsson Enterprise.
3 This information was provided by Mr. Hideo Nishijima, director of management control department at Ricoh Corporation, through Professor Takeo Yoshikawa.
4 This information was provided by Xerox through Jan Roy.
5 This information was provided by Mr. Hiroyuki Tsuruga, president of ATOM Transportation Co., Ltd, through Professor Takeo Yoshikawa.

8

Key Concepts and Thinkers

Short definitions of approximately 40 concepts relating to balanced scorecards.

Action plan

The action plan is the most concrete part of the scorecard. It describes the specific actions and steps that will be required in the future to achieve the goals and the vision that have been established. Like any plan, responsibilities and deadlines need to be assigned. Some companies have made it mandatory to attach revised action plans to any updated scorecard report, even publishing these on the intranet.

Activity-based costing (ABC)

A business practice in which costs are assigned to cost objects through a careful analysis of all activities. ABC provides useful information for deciding on the activities described in a scorecard, as it provides better estimates than standard absorption costing of the cost of different alternatives.

Balance

In the balanced scorecard, we are referring to several different kinds of balance:

» the balance between the short and the long term;
» the balance between the four perspectives;
» the balance between measuring change and the situation at a particular time – similar to the difference between a profit statement and a balance sheet; and
» the balance between how others see us (perspective) and how we see ourselves (focus).

As a description of business activities, measures should cover all of these. Based on the inherent logic in the scorecard, targets should be set which reflect all these balances.

Balanced scorecard

A strategic, measurement-based management system, proposed by Robert Kaplan and David Norton, which provides a method of aligning business activities to the strategy, and monitoring performance of strategic goals over time. Originally, a balanced scorecard is a format for communication about activities consisting of four perspectives, each of which should include a small number of important metrics. These should be linked through the business logic inherent in the strategy.

Benchmarking

The process of comparing one set of measurements to another, especially those which represent good practice. This may be done for various reasons, such as to determine trends in a process over time, or to compare the efficiency of one organization with another. In the context of scorecards, there is sometimes a conflict between the ambition to select more general metrics that permit this kind of comparison, and more specific metrics that are more relevant to the particular situation but for which no comparisons can be made.

Bonus

Compensation systems may use performance as measured on scorecards as a vital component. Formal links between the scorecard and bonuses often take the form of weighting the measurements. This carries the danger of employees focusing too much on measures that are easy to improve, contradicting the idea of a "balance". Bonuses may also be linked to scorecards in more complex ways, for instance requiring certain "threshold" values to be met before any bonus is awarded, and then tying a bonus to only some of the measures.

Business logic; business model

The activities of an organization should be based on some idea about how it will have an impact on, and be received by, all important stakeholders, maybe also including its ecological setting, and about the consequent interplay between the organization and its environment. For businesses pursuing profit, this idea should in a credible way answer the question of *why* the company expects to achieve long-term success. Sometimes the business logic may be implicit. It may not be shared by all observers, but to create motivation it is usually necessary that managers and vital employees share a conviction that this "business logic", sometimes summarized in a "business model", is credible and suited to the resources of the company.

For non-profit making activities, we may also talk about a similar "logic". For instance, in preventing crime the police will have to make assumptions about the impact of and reactions from their activities. Scorecards, and strategy maps, in particular, are useful ways of articulating and communicating business models. Cf. cause and effect relationships!

The authors do not find it necessary to distinguish very precisely between the concepts of "business logic" and "strategy". Although the latter usually carries implications of a prescription of specific activities, these should be based on (business) logic.

Cause and effect relationships

One of the challenges when creating a balanced scorecard is to establish cause and effect relationships (links) between measures, both within and between perspectives. To some extent, any business strategy is a risky bet that our current endeavors will be rewarded through future events. Such causal reasoning should be articulated in a scorecard – *hypotheses* about the future. Scorecards will also include some causes and effects that we believe have been shown by experience to be true, or even logically necessary. Over time, hypotheses then are replaced by *accepted knowledge*.

Critical success factors (CSFs)

The most critical factors for the company's success in achieving its strategic aims and vision. When developing scorecards, a key element is to identify CSFs for the strategy in each perspective, and then to derive suitable measures and action plans from them.

Customer perspective

One of the original four perspectives used to create a balanced scorecard. This perspective describes how customers experience the services they receive, and their attitude in general to the firm. It has been described as "how our customers view us", but it may also be important to include "how we view our customers", that is, do we reach our target audience, or have we established the loyalty we wish for, for example. When using a scorecard to describe some business activity, the customer perspective captures the external perception of the activity, and its links to the environment.

Customer satisfaction indices

During the 1990s, institutes were created in some countries to measure and compare customer satisfaction among different industries and companies. Usually expressed on a scale one through 100, such measures are often combined with additional information about what features of the products or services are judged to be important by customers.

EFQM

The European Foundation for Quality Management (EFQM) has established a model of excellence, which provides benchmarking and self-assessment in a framework similar to that of the Malcolm Baldrige criteria. EFQM issues the European Quality Award. There are similar organizations and distinctions in a number of countries. These criteria cover aspects of a company which often turn up in scorecards, making quality projects comparable to scorecard projects. Use of the EFQM and similar models is a good preparation for scorecard work. However, "excellence" here is a more general concept than the strategic uniqueness which should be the goal when scorecards are used as a tool for strategic management. "Quality" and "excellence" are difficult to define when applied to renewal and growth activities, and choosing the right direction for these is essentially a matter of future vision, not benchmarking against others. Because of this, quality projects is no substitute for scorecards.

EVA™

Economic value added (EVA) is a trademark held by Stern Stewart & Co. EVA is the residual income remaining after operating profits cover the cost of capital. It is calculated (at least in principle) by first recognizing a company's spending on intangibles (R&D, marketing, etc.) over past years as investments. This will give both a corrected value for profits, and an increased capital base (now including intangible investments). A capital charge is then calculated as a percentage of this capital base, using a cost of capital appropriate for the degree of risk. This capital charge is then deducted from the revised profit value. Only if a company (or a unit within a company) shows a surplus is it considered to "add value".

The advantage of EVA is that it is logically coherent with discounted cash flow as a decision rule for investments, and treats material and immaterial investments in a similar way. Basing rewards on EVA should then induce managers to produce optimal value for shareholders. Although fundamentally sound, this argument neglects the need for certain businesses, especially units within companies, to pursue (at least temporarily) other strategic objectives than profit, in the interest of synergies or other corporate goals. These would be better served by the use of balanced scorecards as part of management control. Scorecards could, of course, incorporate EVA as a metric. If calculated correctly, it should provide a better indication of long-term profits than accounting profit. But calculating correct EVAs is not always easy, and many users of scorecards believe this effort to be unproductive.

Financial perspective

A perspective in the original format for devising balanced scorecards. This perspective should show the results of the strategic choices made in the other perspectives, whilst establishing several of the long-term goals and thus a large part of the general ground rules and premises for the other perspectives. Using a scorecard to describe some business activity, the financial perspective captures how it fulfills the objectives set by the owners – or, for non-profit making activities, the instigators of the activity.

Focus

Some organizations prefer the term "focus" or "focus area" to the term "perspective". There may be a slight difference of meaning. The customer perspective is about our company as customers see us: a minimum of delays, a pleasant feeling about nice products, or a good product line. A customer focus, on the other hand, may be about customers as we see them. For example, what is the market penetration of our products in different age groups or industries? Is the number of our customers increasing? Are we vulnerable from selling to a limited number of major customers?

Goals

See Targets.

Human resource perspective

Some organizations have added a fifth perspective, related to human resource factors that are considered strategically important. Sometimes also called "employee focus", it may be useful in stressing the importance of human resources in a company's strategy. Some argue, however, that this goal will be better served by using employee-related metrics in the other perspectives – after all, employees should be important as part of processes, development work, and meeting customers. They see a danger that the scorecard may become a stakeholder model, which is not its basic logic.

Individual scorecards

Some organizations seek to break their scorecards down all the way to the individual level. This step is most natural, of course, when employees are fairly autonomous and are supposed to cultivate customer contacts or special competencies, for example. It may also be necessary when individual rewards are to be linked to the balanced scorecards of a company.

Intellectual capital

Different writers have interpreted this term in varying ways, but the most frequent meaning is "packaged useful knowledge", which is assumed to be the reason why an organization is valued more than the sum of the "hard" assets in the balance sheet. Knowledge here has to be construed as a very broad concept. Processes, information systems, unreleased new products, brand names, employee skills, and customer files may all be part of intellectual capital. A large part of the motivation for the use of scorecards comes from the growing importance of intellectual capital, which in traditional performance management tends to be visible only as costs. Building and maintaining intellectual capital are often important performance drivers and should be made visible in scorecards. Some divide the intellectual capital into subcategories which they map onto scorecards: "customer capital", "process capital", etc.

Internal/business-process perspective

Another perspective in the original format for devising balanced scorecards. This perspective describes the processes that generate value for customers and lead to the fulfillment of shareholder expectations. Using a scorecard to describe a business activity, this perspective describes its ongoing, internal "machinery".

ISO

The European standards organization, ISO, has established a series of performance and quality measurement procedures for industrial organizations; if they implement these procedures they may receive certification by ISO. Companies using such measures may find it natural to use some of them in their scorecards as well.

Kaplan, R.S.

Robert S. Kaplan is a professor of accounting at Harvard Business School and (with Norton) the originator of the balanced scorecard concept.

Key performance indicators (KPI)

A particular value or characteristic used to measure output or outcome. As early as the 1960s, it was suggested that critical success factors could be identified and then specified in the form of key performance indicators or key numbers. Sometimes a comparison is built into a KPI by dividing two numbers (key ratio).

Learning and growth perspective

Another perspective in the original format for devising balanced scorecards. The learning and growth perspective enables an organization to ensure its capacity for long-term renewal, a prerequisite for survival in the long run. Using a scorecard to describe a business activity, this perspective describes the effort performed during a particular time period to change its internal processes, its links to external parties (especially customers), or its financial circumstances.

Learning organization

The long-term function of the scorecard can be regarded as developing a learning organization that is constantly developing and changing in a way that will keep the company competitive in the future. Cf. cause and effect: scorecards should depict expectations about how our activities will be rewarded in the longer run. By using scorecards to monitor our progress, we gradually learn more about these linkages.

Links

See cause and effect relationships.

Measures

Measures are compact descriptions of observations, summarized in numbers or words. A balanced scorecard contains measures that have been developed to enable management to exploit the success factors considered most critical for goal achievement. The word measurement often refers to a particular observed value, while we use measure or metric to denote a specific scale for measuring. In each perspective, the number of measures should not be too large – three to five are often suggested as suitable. However, among these there should be a good mix of performance drivers and outcome measures.

Norton, D.P.

David P. Norton is president of the Balanced Scorecard Collaborative and (with Kaplan) the originator of the balanced scorecard concept.

Outcome measures

In a balanced scorecard, a distinction can be made between "performance drivers", that is, measures that describe resources spent or activities performed, and "outcome measures". Usually a mixture is desired, as the former should act as early indicators of future outcomes, and we also want to clarify causes and effects through showing links between drivers and outcomes. Sometimes there may be long chains of causes and effects. We may, for example, want to measure the outcomes of a development project as a part of the scorecard's "learning and growth" perspective, and this in turn may be seen as an input for marketing or production, that is, "internal processes". This means that it sometimes is difficult to draw the line between drivers and outcomes. For people in charge of logistics, delivery time is an outcome, but for purposes of customer relations it may be considered as one of several performance drivers that can improve customer loyalty.

Also cf. cause and effect relationships.

Performance drivers

See outcome measures.

Performance management

The term used to indicate management control based on performance measures corresponding roughly to a scorecard's financial perspective – usually stressing profitability (ROI) as the main goal for a business unit. Recently, software vendors use enterprise performance management (and similar terms) for an integrated system providing all kinds of measures used in management control – ie, including those in balanced scorecards.

Perspective

In a balanced scorecard, the overall vision is described in terms of a number of perspectives. The most frequently used perspectives are the shareholder and financial perspective, the customer perspective, the internal/business-process perspective, and a learning and growth perspective. Certain organizations have added a separate employee or human resource perspective.

Strategic aims

In a scorecard, the vision is expressed as a number of more specific strategic aims, one (or sometimes a few) for each perspective. These serve to guide the company in achieving its vision. From the strategies, a number of critical success factors and measures are developed.

Strategic management

A term sometimes used for management control where the intention is to capture the strategic aims of business units, usually combining both financial and non-financial metrics. Balanced scorecards belong to this category.

Strategy

According to a dictionary (Merriam – Webster), "a careful plan or method especially for achieving an end". In management literature, it has often been reserved for the principles guiding more long-term activities, and short-term activities expected to have long-term effects. To identify these in a precise way is often difficult, and as for many other words that have been used in varying contexts for a long time we find it unproductive to insist on any more specific meaning.

Business strategy usually refers to a particular business (business unit) – see business logic and business model. *Corporate* strategy refers to an entire corporation (group of businesses). It should explain the logic of grouping these together, also indicating how the group as an entity should be developed.

Strategy maps

One way of illustrating scorecards, highlighting cause and effect linkages, is called strategy maps. For illustrations see Figure 3.1 and Figure 6.4.

Targets

The terms "aims", "goals", and "objectives" are used without precise distinctions. "Target" refers to a particular value for some metric, which has been agreed during a planning process that a business unit should achieve. Targets should always be set with clear accountability and a determined time frame.

Scorecards are used to document both plans and what was actually achieved. A scorecard plan will include targets for up to 20 measures.

As the scorecard documents a desired "balance" between these, it is not obvious how the responsible manager (or team) should prioritize if all targets cannot be met. The cause and effect logic of the scorecard should provide some clues. Ideally, there should be an ongoing dialog within the organization, adapting plans as conditions change.

Total quality management (TQM)

This term is often used for the range of different initiatives and methods that have been developed during the past 30 years for improving and controlling processes in industry and administration. It is heavily based on quantitative measures. In many countries there are quality organizations promoting more systematic attention to quality, and especially in industry, many companies have introduced special systems and officers for managing quality. These often prove very useful in balanced scorecard projects, although at times a certain rivalry may be experienced. See EFQM.

Value-based management

A term sometimes used for management control based on performance measures which are meant to link better to value creation (usually in the sense of shareholder value) than traditional ones (see "performance management"), but which are still largely monetary or derived from financial numbers. One example is EVA. Some companies try to use such new metrics as part of the financial perspective in scorecards.

Vision

By vision we mean the desired future situation of an organization. The purpose of the vision is to guide, control, and challenge an entire organization towards realizing a shared conception of the company in the future.

9

Resources

A listing of books, articles, reports, and websites containing information for the study of balanced scorecards.

Below are presented some resources for those who would like to investigate the balanced scorecard concept further. The treatment of the balanced scorecard should, however, not be seen in isolation. Related areas of interest include performance measures, management control, business strategy, strategy development, strategic planning, strategy implementation, knowledge management, intellectual capital, and quality management.

BOOKS

The three books by Robert S. Kaplan and David P. Norton and published by Harvard Business School Press are basic for an understanding of the concept:

» *The Balanced Scorecard: Translating Strategy into Action* (1996). Describes a form of balanced scorecard based primarily on measure selection, built around early cases carried out by David Norton in conjunction with Gemini Consulting and others.

» *The Strategy-Focused Organization: How Balanced Scorecard Companies Thrive in the New Business Environment* (2000). Kaplan and Norton explain how companies such as Mobil, CIGNA, and Chemical Retail Bank have used the balanced scorecard concept for nearly a decade. The book guides readers through the development of strategy maps, implemented throughout the enterprise and made an integral part of its future. The authors show how companies have linked long-term strategy with operational and budgetary management, and detail the double loop process for doing so, monitoring progress, and initiating corrective actions if necessary.

» *Strategy Maps: Converting Intangible Assets into Tangible Outcomes* (2004). This third book by the originators of the concept provides numerous examples of firms focusing on how they have articulated their business logic. The examples come from their consulting practice.

The author of the present book collaborated on two larger Wiley books on BSC:

» *Performance Drivers: A Practical Guide to Using the Balanced Scorecard* by Nils-Göran Olve, Jan Roy and Magnus Wetter, John Wiley & Sons, 1999 (paperback edition 2000)

The book provides a step-by-step method for introducing the balanced scorecard into an organization. This is done through the use of practical examples, with numerous case studies. The desired strategic control system using scorecards that is presented focuses on creating and communicating a comprehensive picture to all members of the organization from the top down, a long-term view of what the company's strategic objectives really are, how to make use of knowledge gained through experience and the required flexibility of such a system to cope with the fast-changing business environment.

» *Making Scorecards Actionable* by Nils-Göran Olve, Carl-Johan Petri, Jan Roy and Sofie Roy. Wiley 2003

Explores how 15 firms went about introducing scorecards, identifying pitfalls and success factors. Six main issues in designing scorecard projects are discussed, indicating the necessity for practitioners to choose what kind of scorecard use they aim for.

Two books focusing workforce strategies may be recommended (both Harvard Business School Press):

» *The HR Scorecard: Linking People, Strategy, and Performance* by Brian E. Becker, Mark A. Huselid and Dave Ulrich (2001). The book is based on a study of approximately 3000 firms and outlines a seven-step process called the HR Scorecard, designed to incorporate human resources' systems in a firm's overall strategy. It also shows how to link human resources' results to measures such as profitability and shareholder value. The authors argue that human resources' strategic role begins with designing the HR architecture – the HR function, the HR system, and strategic employee behaviors – that emphasizes and reinforces the implementation of the firm's strategy.

» *The Workforce Scorecard* by Mark A. Huselid, Brian E. Becker and Richard W. Beatty (2005). The authors propose a workforce scorecard as a link between the HR scorecards they discussed in their previous book and corporate balanced scorecards.

Some other recommended books are:

» *Performance Measurement & Control Systems for Implementing Strategy: Text & Cases* by Robert Simons, Antonio Davila and Robert S. Kaplan, Prentice Hall College Div., 1999

The book presents control system tools and techniques that are needed to manage a business effectively. It presents new accounting techniques, including profit wheel analysis, and strategic profitability analysis, and provides a comprehensive presentation of the balanced scorecard approach.

» *Balanced Scorecard in the Federal Government* by James B. Whittaker, Management Concepts, Inc., 2000

The book describes how to adjust the balanced scorecard concept for implementation in the federal government, in order to achieve full compliance with the US Government Performance and Results Act of 1993.

» *The Consultant's Scorecard: Tracking Results and Bottom-Line Impact of Consulting Projects* by Jack Phillips, McGraw-Hill, 2000

The author presents a model to measure the success of consulting projects in terms of business impact, ROI, and other performance measures. The book shows both consultants and clients how they can track and measure the success of consulting and performance improvement projects. According to the author, by collecting the right data during and after a consulting intervention, it is possible to create a complete profile of project success.

ARTICLES

Robert S. Kaplan and David P. Norton have written numerous articles in *Harvard Business Review*, together and with other authors. Often these have preceded books with similar contents, cf. above. Here are their most important articles for that magazine:

» The balanced scorecard – measures that drive performance (Jan-Feb. 1992)
» Putting the balanced scorecard to work (Sep-Oct 1993)
» Using the balanced scorecard as a strategic management system (Jan-Feb 1996)

» Having Trouble with Your Strategy? Then Map It (Sep 2000)
» Measuring the Strategic Readiness of Intangible Assets (Feb 2004)

Some other articles are:

Epstein, M.J. and Manzoni, J.-F. (1997) The balanced scorecard & tableau de bord: a global perspective on translating strategy into action. *INSEAD Working Paper* 97/63/AC/SM.

Epstein, M. and Manzoni, J.-F. (1998) Implementing corporate strategy: from tableaux de bord to balanced scorecards. *European Management Journal* **16**, 2, 190–203.

To use "tableaux de bord" is a French practice: a dashboard or instrument panel for management, consisting of selected metrics. In most cases, it would seem to be less consciously linked to strategy than balanced scorecards. As a precursor to scorecards, it has nevertheless attracted interest recently.

Dinesh, D. and Palmer, E. (1998) Management by objectives and the balanced scorecard: will Rome fall again? *Management Decision*, **36**, 6, 363–9.

Mooray, S., Oyon, D. and Hostettler, D. (1999) The balanced scorecard: a necessary good or an unnecessary evil? *European Management Journal* **17**, 5, 481–491.

Barsky, N.P. and Bremser, W.G. (1999) Performance measurement, budgeting and strategic implementation in the multinational enterprise. *Managerial Finance*, **25**, 2, 3ff.

Lipe, M.G. and Salterio, S.E. (2000) The balanced scorecard: judgemental effects of common and unique performance measures. *The Accounting Review*, **75**, 3, 283–298.

Frimansson, L. and Lind, J. (2001) The balanced scorecard and learning in business relationships. *Business Network Learning*, 32–52.

Aidemark, L-G. (2001) The meaning of balanced scorecards in the health care organization. *Financial Accountability & Management*, **17**, 1 (Feb), 23–40.

Nørreklit, H. (2003) The Balanced Scorecard: what is the score? – A rhetorical analysis of the Balanced Scorecard. *Accounting, Organizations and Society* **28**, 591–619

Mouritsen, J., Thorsgaard Larsen, H. and Bukh, P.N. (2005) Dealing with the knowledge economy: intellectual capital versus balanced scorecard. *Journal of Intellectual Capital* **6**, 1

Ax, C. and Bjørnenak, T. (2005) Bundling and diffusion of management accounting innovations – the case of the balanced scorecard in Sweden. *Management Accounting Research* **16**, 1, 1–20

The above articles are examples of how the interest of the business world in scorecards has, in turn, attracted the intention of researchers who try to understand the phenomenon and judge its prospects.

Nilsson, F. and Olve, N-G. (2001) On control systems in multibusiness companies: from performance management to strategic management. *European Management Journal* **19**, 4, 344–358. This article, co-written by one of the authors of this book, expands the discussion at the end of Chapter 2, discussing the usefulness of performance management, value-based management, and strategic management under different circumstances, and also their demands on an organization.

REPORTS

» "Transforming Strategic Performance through the Balanced Scorecard: How to Drive Effective Strategy Alignment and Execution", by Chris Ashton, Business Intelligence, 2001, www.business-intelligence.co.uk

   This report contains information from a wide range of balanced scorecard users. It describes how they have evolved and adapted the basic idea.

» "A Business Performance Scorecard for HR", The Concours Group, 2000, www.concoursgroup.com

   This report provides the tools to adequately measure specific human resources (HR) activities and outcomes as a means of helping senior executives to monitor the performance and the business value of HR. A "business performance scorecard" demonstrates the contribution of HR to the business and helps to ensure that the attention and efforts of HR professionals will remain focused on important business priorities.

» "Implementing an IT Performance Scorecard", The Concours Group, 2000, www.concoursgroup.com

   The report looks at IT performance measurement, drawing on techniques for measuring customer satisfaction, and business results in service organizations. The results are structured as a "dashboard" for steering the course of an IT organization and communicating its performance, in business terms, to the CEO, and the executive team.

WEBSITES

» The Balanced Scorecard Collaborative – www.bscol.com

The Balanced Scorecard Collaborative (BSCol) is a professional services firm specializing in balanced scorecard research and consultancy. The Collaborative was founded by David Norton and Robert Kaplan.

» The Balanced Scorecard Institute – www.balancedscorecard.org

The Balanced Scorecard Institute is an independent, non-profit making source of information about applications of the balanced scorecard approach to management in government and other non-profit making organizations.

» Better Management – www.bettermanagement.com

Better Management provides resources on up to date performance management topics, including balanced scorecards. The site includes a forum, links, articles, papers, audio clips, and a newsletter.

» Charlotte's Balanced Scorecard – www.ci.charlotte.nc.us/cibudget/score.htm

This site provides an example of a balanced scorecard in practice for a non-profit making organization, describing the development of a balanced scorecard by the City of Charlotte.

» Foundation for Performance Measurement – www.fpm.com

The Foundation is a membership organization that serves as a source of information, a forum for research and debate, and as a link to tools and resources for organizations interested in new ways of measuring enterprise performance.

Ten Steps to Making Balanced Scorecards Work

A collection of five suggested pieces of advice for the initial development process, and five areas to consider during the period after the introduction of scorecards. In conclusion, some final words of wisdom.

How management will proceed in implementing and using the balanced scorecard concept depends on a number of factors: the maturity of the industry, the age of the organization, organizational culture, existing systems of management control, and the age profile of company staff, for example. In other words, it is very difficult to generalize. However, certain aspects considered essential to a project's success may be highlighted.

ADVICE FOR THE INITIAL DEVELOPMENT PROCESS

There are several factors that can contribute to the success or potential failure in the phase of building the initial scorecards. Below are presented the most important ones. However, once again it must be stressed that this work is a continuous process, and not an isolated initial effort that is being made just to create a balanced scorecard.

1. Support and participation

Without the firm support of top management, it is extremely difficult to succeed in implementing balanced scorecards. Also, it takes a long time before the entire organization will understand both the ideas involved in the concept and its impact on the daily work of individual employees. During this time it is of utmost importance for the entire organization to feel that top management unreservedly endorses the values, ideas, and management philosophy inherent in the concept.

As already stated, one of the primary tasks is to establish participation and communication concerning the vision and strategic aims of an organization. If the balanced scorecard concept is applied improperly, people in the organization view it as a tool to check on them rather than to ensure that the company is making progress toward its established goals. Of course there is an element of this in any control system. In most modern companies introducing scorecards, however, the emphasis is much more on creating agreement about direction, rather than on checking compliance with orders from top management. We have seen that it is important that a large part of the organization participates in the actual process of developing the balanced scorecard, a process that begins with the comprehensive vision of the organization. In this way consensus may be reached as to how each individual can help the organization to achieve its strategic objectives. Again, we have seen that much time will be saved later in the process if resources and time are allocated at an early stage to discuss the ideas and involve people.

It is also critical that top management be able to explain the purpose of the project and its relationship to previous projects in the organization. For example, if the organization has already worked with multidimensional measures as part of TQM, management should build on this experience and show what scorecards can add.

To reiterate, it is impossible to give an organization too much information and training. It is essential that information on the balanced scorecard concept be readily available and easily understood. Training and information can be provided with the help of manuals, an intranet, or seminars. Experience has shown that information is transmitted most easily to groups of 20 people or less. In larger groups, people may be more reluctant to ask questions and critically examine the ideas underlying the concept.

2. Composition of the project group

Again, we have seen that the balanced scorecard concept is intended to provide as complete a picture as possible of the organization. Therefore, many different parts of the organization should be represented in the project group, and contribute their views during the process of developing the balanced scorecard. For instance, in some organizations it was felt that too many members of the project group had their professional background in accounting. Not surprisingly, there was a tendency among them to favor the use of traditional financial measures.

It is impossible to generalize about an optimal size of the project group. Although it is important not to let the group grow so large that efficiency and freedom of action are impaired, it should not be so small that certain parts of the organization have no voice in the process.

As we have seen, many companies use consultants to guide them through the initial stage. They can provide experience from scorecard projects for other organizations, they can question "received wisdom" about strategies and business logics, and add capacity for handling the workload of the project. But, we have seen that it is important to realize that – even more than with other management methods – scorecard projects have to reflect local conditions and be "owned" by people in the organization. This means that consultants should act as facilitators and not submit to the temptation to impose ready-made models.

3. Coverage of the project

If a balanced scorecard project is too broad in coverage (remember the case of Xerox) and/or involves too many people, there is a danger that the work will balloon and overtax the resources of the organization. It may then take too much time to gain the necessary support for the concept, and the effects desired may not be obtained. Also, the project may consume so much of the time of key personnel that seeing it through to the finish is perceived as burdensome. As we have seen (Ericsson Enterprise) some organizations seek to avoid this danger by starting with a pilot project at a subsidiary or department. The organization can then learn from its mistakes and have an easier time with further implementation of the concept. Another advantage of a pilot project is that it can help win the confidence of employees. What employees like and dislike about the concept may carry more weight than the pronouncements of top management or outsiders.

However, some companies believe in company-wide implementation of the concept from the very outset (see the Ricoh case study), reasoning that the concept raises issues with broader ramifications. This approach forces the entire company to change its philosophy of management control, and to look ahead to its goals for the future. The drawback is that the process – gaining support, spreading the message, and instilling appropriate attitudes – may take a very long time.

4. Basing the balanced scorecard on the strategy of the organization

It cannot be emphasized enough that it is fundamental that the balanced scorecard be based on the comprehensive vision and overall strategic aims of the organization. Before a balanced scorecard process can go further, the strategy of the organization must be broken down into measures and goals consistent with these. If the scorecard is not based on strategy, there is a serious danger of suboptimization, with different parts of the organization working at cross-purposes. The principal challenge is to achieve a balance between maximum participation in the process of strategy formulation, and maintaining focus on operations. Experience has shown that many enjoy dreaming of a distant vision more than coming to grips with their day-to-day work. For that reason some organizations (see ATOM Transportation) have chosen to entrust the process of strategy formulation to a small group, whereas the rest of the organization formulates business plans, devises measures, and sets targets.

5. Relationship to existing control systems

The balanced scorecard is a method for strategic control of a business or other operations. Naturally, it must be aligned with existing systems of control, particularly management control. Budgets, reports, and incentive systems must be adapted to the balanced scorecard process and in time co-ordinated, perhaps even integrated, with the measures used in scorecards. Otherwise, traditional responsibility and rewards for monetary performance will probably continue to predominate, at the expense of responsibility for successfully meeting the commitments that have emerged from the dialog. In addition, the administrative processes will be unnecessarily costly.

To rely entirely on scorecards for management control may seem worrisome, even dangerous, to management, particularly at the corporate level (board of directors and senior corporate management). As explained in Figure 2.2, the customary view of the business at this level is often in terms of financial measures. This description may be the only possible one at the top level of a diversified organization that operates in different industries and thus serves a variety of markets. Quite early in the development process, an organization must clearly state the desired combination of monetary and non-monetary responsibility for its managers. It needs to define its own mixture of performance management, value-based management and strategic management, and adapt this to different business units and different levels of the organizational hierarchy.

ISSUES IN THE CONTINUOUS PROCESS

6. Setting goals and monitoring progress

Goals must be set for each measure. They may change over time, depending on the situation, and the timeframe in question. But, again, if a balanced scorecard is to be credible, goals must first be consistent with the comprehensive vision and overall strategy of the organization. Second, they must be realistic and attainable. Although goals must be ambitious enough to spur the organization to develop, it is also important that employees throughout the organization find that most goals are met.

We have suggested that a organization needs both short-term and long-term goals. Short-term goals should have a timeframe of three to 18 months, and they may constitute subgoals in relation to a long-term goal. To maintain focus on measures related to short-term goals, measurements should be taken relatively often, perhaps even monthly. In contrast, long-term goals cover a period of two to five years, and they are commonly updated and modified during the process of strategy formulation. To function as instruments of control, measurements of progress toward long-term goals must be taken at least once a year, and preferably each quarter.

7. Clearly defined measures and methods of measurement

We have seen that the measures used in a balanced scorecard should be defined precisely and in the same way throughout the organization. If an organization wishes to compare the progress of different subsidiaries and/or departments, it must be clear from the start when formulating common definitions for the measures to be used. The definitions should also be easily accessible, in a database or manual, for example. If it is too difficult to find a measure, there is a danger that this will be an excuse for not implementing any measurement at all.

If a balanced scorecard is to be effective, it must be continually filled with current, relevant information so that it becomes a natural part of the strategic discussion and learning of an organization. The process of formulating the balanced scorecard often results in a number of measures that do not exist among the present systems of the organization. Here, the project group must ensure that the necessary data will be provided. Otherwise the organization may well find itself with a balanced scorecard filled with a number of measures that cannot be followed. It will then be difficult to achieve a learning organization and to test strategy.

The organization must therefore develop intuitive, flexible, and cost-effective systems and procedures for measurement, systems which will make it possible to use information from available databases – both internal and external – and which also permit the automation of measurement that has been performed manually in the normal course of operations.

8. Balance and cause and effect relationships between measures

We have outlined how organizational objectives have traditionally been expressed in terms of financial measures and goals. As a result, systems have been developed to permit the monitoring of financial measures virtually on a daily basis. Many organizations lack the capability to monitor non-financial measures, or have no tradition of doing so; here, there is a substantial risk that non-financial measures will be neglected. A balanced scorecard is intended not only to give an organization a broader view of its business but also to force it to determine how the different measures affect each other.

As we have discussed, scorecards provide a good opportunity to learn from experience, gradually converting our hypotheses about how drivers will affect outcomes into confirmed knowledge about such linkages. Even if an organization has no historical statistics on causation, it is essential that they be discussed within the organization. When cause and effect relationships cannot (yet) be verified, management must still have some ideas about them. We emphasized customer-sustaining activities, service, or development of competence because they are presumed to benefit future business and increase future profits. The desirable "balance" in a balanced scorecard depends entirely on such assumptions.

9. IT-based presentation and support systems

Many people believe that an organization cannot reap the full benefits from balanced scorecards unless they are linked to an IT-based presentation and support system. With computer-based diagrams and illustrations, an organization can quickly and easily obtain a comprehensive view of how it is doing. In this way individuals can clearly see the impact of their work on the overall performance of the organization. Although an IT-based presentation and support system is required if data collection and reporting is to function in the long term, it is also important that the balanced scorecard project does not acquire an image as a "computer project" too early in the process. If it does, it may be considered too abstract by many people in the organization.

We have seen that how much IT support should be used, and at what stage of the balanced scorecard process, are questions to be decided from case to case. Clearly, a larger organization with more operating units will have different needs than a smaller company with more concentrated operations. Nevertheless, interesting opportunities are now emerging for utilizing IT support in a more standardized way, and at acceptable cost, in particular for the strategic discussions of top management on linking different factors and measures.

10. Developing the learning organization

In the balanced scorecard process, strategy is broken down into measures and specific goals. This process develops participation, aware-ness, a decentralized decision-making process, and responsibility for achieving the goals that have been formulated. As a consequence, there must be a goal-achievement analysis, in which the organization draws conclusions about what it is doing well, what it is not doing so well, and what can be improved. Here, more or less formalized simulations and scenario models may be of interest as management tools.

To remain competitive, an organization must constantly review its strategy. Most organizations operate in an environment that compels them to test their strategy continually. The link between the strategic aims of the organization and the measures in its balanced scorecard may be regarded as a hypothesis of certain cause and effect relationships. If, later, there turns out to be no correlation between measures and strategic aims, this is an indication that the hypotheses underlying the choice of strategy should be re-examined. Discussions of this kind should be held at least once a year, perhaps even on a quarterly or monthly basis. A balanced scorecard should not be regarded as a static product but as a living model of an organization.

FINAL WORDS

In this chapter we have discussed ten steps, or rather ten issues that are vitally important for successful scorecard projects. They are "steps" in the sense that they will appear and require management attention in roughly this order. But, they need to be handled continuously over time. To become an avenue towards improved management control, the balanced scorecard process is better regarded as a never-ending circle (see Fig. 10.1, which reuses Fig. 6.5 to provide a graphic image of a danger to be avoided – that of the interrupted process). We have been sad to see this happen several times. Some organizations have been able to restart their process later. Some claim that they reaped enough benefits from the early stages of the process: a clearer understanding of their strategy, better communicated than before. Still, it was a lost opportunity not to carry on.

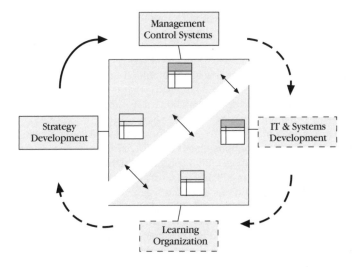

Fig. 10.1   Breaking the process circle.

As a condition for success we would particularly emphasize the importance of the virtuous circle formed by strategy, control, measurement, learning, and back to strategy. If the circle is broken, much of the potential of the balanced scorecard will be lost; on the other hand, if the circle is kept intact, the continuous process will enable organizations to benefit from a combination of some of the most significant elements of modern management control.

Frequently Asked Questions (FAQs)

Q1: What is a balanced scorecard?

A: See Chapter 2!

Q2: Can you suggest some good metrics for my scorecards?

A: Scorecards should assist in developing a strategic uniqueness – so metrics need to be highly customized. For more general advice read "On non-financial measures" in Chapter 2 and "Requirements for measures" in Chapter 6, then look at the figures in chapters 2, 3, 6 and 7!

Q3: How can scorecards be used in management control?

A: As a tool in discussing activities, agreeing on ambitions, monitoring achievements, and rewarding good performance. See the final sections of Chapter 2 and Chapter 3; "Management control or merely performance measurement?" in Chapter 6; "Relationship to existing control systems" and "Issues in the continuous process" in Chapter 10, and the experiences of the case companies in Chapter 7.

Q4: Must we do it all – is there some "light" version to start with?

A: The extent and coverage of projects vary. Some organizations even feel that they benefit from just the use of scorecards for *some* units, and just for discussing strategy rather than as the full-blown control system advocated. See also "Appropriate levels in the organization" in Chapter 6, "Variants" and "Applications" in Chapter 3, and "Coverage of the project" in Chapter 10. But watch out for the danger that what is intended as a strategic control system ends up as just performance measurement – see "Final words" in Chapter 10!

Q5: Do we really need to involve people in discussions about our strategy?

A: See Chapter 1, and the case studies in Chapter 7! Some managers are embarrassed because they sense that their strategies are not well articulated to begin with. Our experience is that scorecard projects often result in improved strategies, not just the communication of existing ones. This is one reason why strategy maps (cf. Figure 3.1 and Figure 6.4) are gaining in importance.

Q6: Shouldn't we first procure the software we are going to use for scorecards?

A: See Chapter 4!

Q7: Isn't profit what counts in the long run after all?

A: An organization's scorecard should show how current activities support long-term profitability. To emphasize short-term profits is rarely wise. See Chapter 1 about the importance of developing intangible assets, which is usually accounted for as expenses. Trade-offs in the scorecard will, of course, reflect current business necessities – see the KappAhl case study in Chapter 7!

Q8: Should scorecards be linked to bonuses?

A: See "Will scorecards have any impact without new reward systems" in Chapter 6!

Q9: Are scorecards useful outside industry?

A: See "Use in government and other non-profit making organizations" in Chapter 6! Recognizing that long-term aims are different, most of our discussion is equally valid for such organizations.

Q10: Who should be in charge of scorecard projects?

A: See "Responsibilities for scorecards" in Chapter 6. Experience suggests that strong involvement from top executives is needed – see the KappAhl case study (Chapter 7) and "Support and participation" and "Composition of the project group" (Chapter 10).

Index